Doing Critical Literacy

Compellin   ow to do
critical lite   an be
adapted to   e, it brings
critical lite   eracy that
takes seric   its readers
to the soci   key
questions   rved, who
benefits, v   The
practical a

Extending   r with a
rich range   into
practice, *Doing Critical Literacy* is powerful, relevant, and useful for both pre- and
in-service teacher education and for use in schools.

Hilary Janks teaches English language literacy in the School of Education at Wits
University in Johannesburg, South Africa.

Kerryn Dixon lectures Foundation phase students in the School of Education at
Wits University in Johannesburg, South Africa.

Ana Ferreira lectures in English in the School of Education at Wits University in
Johannesburg, South Africa.

Stella Granville has recently retired from Wits University in Johannesburg, South
Africa. She was a teacher and teacher educator for many years. Her research has
been in the areas of critical literacy and academic literacy.

Denise Newfield lectures in the School of Literature, Language and Media at Wits
University in Johannesburg, South Africa.

Language, Culture, and Teaching

Sonia Nieto, Series Editor

Visit www.routledge.com/education for additional information on titles in the Language, Culture, and Teaching series.

Doing Critical Literacy

Texts and Activities for Students and Teachers

Hilary Janks

with

Kerryn Dixon,
Ana Ferreira, Stella Granville
and Denise Newfield

Routledge
Taylor & Francis Group

NEW YORK AND LONDON

First published 2014
by Routledge
711 Third Avenue, New York, NY 10017

Simultaneously published in the UK
by Routledge
2 Park Square, Milton Park, Abingdon, Oxon OX14 4RN

Routledge is an imprint of the Taylor & Francis Group, an informa business

© 2014 Taylor & Francis

Library of Congress Cataloging in Publication Data
Doing critical literacy: texts and activities for students and teachers/
  edited by Hilary Janks; with Kerryn Dixon, Ana Ferreira, Stella Granville,
  Denise Newfield.
    pages cm — (Language, Culture, and Teaching)
    Includes bibliographical references.
    1. Literacy—Study and teaching. 2. Literacy—Social aspects. 3. Power
    (Social sciences) I. Janks, Hilary, editor of compilation. II. Dixon, Kerryn.
  LB1576.D587 2013
    302.2′244--dc23   2012049871

ISBN: 978-0-415-52809-2 (hbk)
ISBN: 978-0-415-52810-8 (pbk)
ISBN: 978-0-203-11862-7 (ebk)

Typeset in Swiss 721
by Florence Production Ltd, Stoodleigh, Devon, UK

Printed and bound in the United States of America by Sheridan Books, Inc. (a Sheridan Group Company).

Contents

The authors

Hilary Janks teaches at the University of the Witwatersrand, Johannesburg, South Africa in the School of Education. She is the editor and an author of the Critical Language Awareness Series and the author of *Literacy and Power* (2010). Her teaching and research are in the areas of language education in multilingual classrooms, mobile and critical literacy. Her work is committed to a search for equity and social justice in contexts of poverty.

Kerryn Dixon lectures in the School of Education at the University of the Witwatersrand, in Johannesburg, South Africa. She is currently head of division of the Foundation phase. Her teaching and research interests are in early literacy, critical literacy and language policy. She is the author of *Literacy, Power and the Schooled Body* (2010), also published by Routledge.

Ana Ferreira lectures in English in the School of Education at the University of the Witwatersrand, Johannesburg, South Africa. Her teaching interests include critical literacy; film, media and popular culture; sociolinguistics, language in education and language methodologies. She has published in the areas of multiliteracies, reconciliation pedagogies, language and identity, and on the productive engagement of difference in educational contexts. Her current research investigates the relationship between subjectivity and pedagogy in classroom discourse.

Stella Granville from the School of Education at the University of the Witwatersrand has been a teacher and teacher educator for many years. Her research has been in the areas of critical literacy and in academic literacy. She has been particularly interested in understanding pedagogies most suited to first-year university students, particularly those for whom English is not their main language. She is an avid reader of the news and has always used newspaper articles and cartoons in her own teaching.

Denise Newfield lectures in the School of Literature, Language and Media at the University of the Witwatersrand, Johannesburg, South Africa. Her key areas of teaching and research are multiliteracies, multimodality, English education and ways of turning barren classrooms into fertile spaces for learning. Her publications include a special edition of *English Studies in Africa* (49.1, 2006) that contains her award-winning article, 'Mobilising and modalising poetry in a Soweto classroom', and 'Multimodality, social justice and becoming a really South African democracy' (2011).

Acknowledgements

I wish to express our heartfelt appreciation to Hildegard Chapman, who worked for over a year to secure the permissions for this book. She remained gracious in the face of the constant changes and people not responding to her emails. Getting permissions is an endless and difficult task that requires careful record keeping, constant follow-ups and sheer doggedness. This book would not have happened without her.

John Janks proofread the entire book in record time. As always he has been thorough and meticulous in making sure that our errors and inaccuracies were eliminated. His support to me has been unwavering, and his help in the last stages of my putting this book together was a gift. We thank him for his care, generosity and commitment to the project. He is my most trusted critic and I rely on his judgement.

Jerry Harste produced the painting which appears on the cover of the book. When he generously offered to do so, we did not hesitate to accept. Matt Sandham kindly gave us permission to reuse illustrations that he had done for the Critical Language Awareness Series. When he was unable to do new illustrations, Daniel Janks agreed to try his hand at illustrating, having failed to persuade me to use a 'real' illustrator. When you look at his drawings, I think you'll agree that I was right to convince him to do the work. My personal favourite is his drawing of the cat chasing the mouse (Figure 4.10).

Naomi Silverman believed in this book from the start. One could not wish for a more intelligent and caring publisher. This book is unusual in many respects and Naomi understood at a first glance what it hoped to achieve.

I also wish to express my indebtedness to the National Research Foundation for the financial support that has made my research possible and to Jabulani Nkosi for managing my research funds needed in connection with this book.

Finally, I wish to thank the authors who have contributed to this book. Denise Newfield and Stella Granville worked with me previously on the Critical Language Awareness Series, published almost twenty years ago. Kerryn Dixon and Ana Ferreira are my colleagues and former students who have taken critical literacy in new directions and who can be trusted to take it into the future.

Hilary Janks
University of the Witwatersrand
August 2012

Introduction

The ability to do critical literacy gives us potent ways of reading, seeing and acting in the world. The texts and activities in this book have been carefully chosen to give you the practice you need to become critically literate.

Once this happens you will understand how important language is in

- the workings of power
- producing our identity positions
- affecting who gets access to opportunities for a better life.

You will see that texts have social effects, that they are designed to recruit us into their version of 'the truth' and that language can be used for both good and ill. Knowing that texts are not neutral, we need to develop ways to see where they are coming from and to recognize their designs on us, their readers.

This is not to suggest that all writers set out to manipulate their readers. When we communicate, we all want people to believe us and agree with us. Our job as listeners or readers is to understand the speaker's or writer's position and to decide whether or not to stand in the same place.

We need to ask critical questions: Who benefits and who is disadvantaged by the position on offer? Who does it include? Who does it exclude? How has the situation or the person or the action been construed? Are there other possible ways of interpreting what took place? What are the possible social consequences of this view of the world? In effect these are all just versions of the key question for critical literacy: *Whose interests are served?*

By focusing on *doing* critical literacy, our aim is to get you started. Our hope is that, once you get the idea, you will quickly begin to find your own texts to examine and local situations to discuss. You will start to question things that you took for granted before. You will begin to notice things that you used to ignore. You will begin to understand that power, access, identity and difference together with the ways in which language are used are all inter-connected. It is this knowledge that can give you agency, the power to take action. Finally, how you use your agency, is also part of what it means to be *doing* critical literacy.

Language is everywhere

Language and how it is used are at the centre of what it means to *do* critical literacy. Language is what distinguishes us as a species and we are bombarded by it. It comes at us in conversations, arguments and love letters; when we hear it on the radio or watch television and movies; we see it on billboards, on walls and on sweet or candy wrappers; we find it in books and magazines and on the internet. We use it on computers, on our cell phones and on blackboards; we use it for research, and text messaging and social networking. When we use language we produce spoken or written *texts* for others to consume.

Texts are partial

Spoken or oral texts are fleeting unless we capture the words with written notes, a recorder or a video camera. In some situations talk can cause problems as without any recording there is no evidence of who said what. That is why in important meetings someone often takes minutes that later have to be ratified, that is agreed to, by everyone who was at the meeting. Minutes become the official record of the meeting, even though they might capture only the decisions, rather than everything that was said. Minutes give us a version of the meeting. You can see this for yourself: next time you have a class meeting or a discussion, have several people take the minutes and then compare them. In what ways are they the same or different?

Even if minutes provide a word-for-word transcript of what was said, they would still not capture the tone of voice used by the different speakers, laughter, body language or the non-verbal reactions of the participants. Likewise, audio recordings give us disembodied sound and video-recording gives a version influenced by where the camera is pointing. Texts are partial—they cannot capture the world as it is. Even the original oral text presents us with only the ideas, beliefs and values of the speakers.

Texts are not neutral
Partial has two meanings and texts are partial in both senses of the word. First, they offer only *a part of* the story and, second, they are partial in the sense that they are *not neutral* but reflect the point of view of the text producer. In this sense *partial* is the opposite of *impartial*. Another way of saying this is that texts are positioned and they work to position their audiences. The starting point for learning to read texts critically is to recognize that all texts are partial re-presentations of the world.

Choices are made by text producers
In the process of re-presenting the world, text-makers have to make many choices. They have to decide what words to use, whether to include adjectives and adverbs, whether to use the present, the past or

the future tense, whether to use sexist or non-sexist pronouns, whether to join sentences or to leave them separate, how to sequence information, whether to be definite or tentative, approving or disapproving.

What all these choices mean is that written and spoken texts are constructed from a range of possible language options. Anything that has been constructed can be *de*-constructed. This *un*making or *un*picking of the text increases our awareness of the choices that the writer or speaker has made. Every choice foregrounds what was selected and hides, silences or backgrounds what was not selected. Focusing on the selections gives us an opportunity to notice them and to think about their effects.

This book will give you the language tools you need to examine texts critically.

Multiple modes for making meaning
However, to 'read' texts we need to understand more than just language. We have already shown how oral texts are affected by how we use our bodies when we speak. The use of the oral mode on television or film includes, in addition, moving images, sound effects, music, colour, facial expressions and so on. This range of modes can also be found, for example, on web-sites. Many printed texts include more visual than verbal material, depending on the genre or kind of text that it is. Each of these different modes requires text producers to choose from a whole range of signs that convey meaning to us.

What makes multi-modality even more complicated is that we have to interpret how these signs work together. Because *Doing Critical Literacy* is a book, print restricts us to working with mainly verbal and visual signs but we have incorporated other kinds of signs where possible.

We have also given you tools for interpreting the use of non-verbal modes.

Are our choices always conscious?

The choices that text producers make are sometimes deliberate and sometimes unconscious but they are never neutral. Spin-doctors, advertisers and poets pay careful attention to the choices they make and their likely effects. By way of contrast, when we speak, we are often focused on *what* we need to communicate and we do not have time to weigh up all the options in order to control *how* we deliver the message. When we concentrate on the meaning it is as if the forms for expressing what we want to say choose themselves. In order for this to happen at speed, we draw on the ways of talking about things and events that are used in our own communities. In this way, our communities' common-sense ways of thinking about the world speak through us and we re-produce them in the texts we create.

These socially constructed ways of speaking and writing of the communities we inhabit are known as *discourses* and they are bound up with the beliefs, values and practices of these communities. These discourses become so natural to us that we forget that they may not be shared by other discourse communities.

Discourse and the individual

The rights of the individual, as seen by different discourses, is a case in point. The individual comes before the group in the United States Declaration of Independence. It offers as a 'self-evident' truth

> that all men are created equal, that they are endowed by their Creator with certain unalienable Rights, that among these are Life, Liberty and the pursuit of Happiness.

Belief in the freedom of the individual also underpins liberal discourse in the West.

In more collectivist societies this view is not self-evident. Many Africans believe in the philosophy of Ubuntu in which 'a person is a person through other people'. Here the group is more important than the individual and sharing and collaboration are valued above competition.

Conventions and appropriateness

In addition to these habits of speaking, thinking, valuing and doing that we embody (discourse), every society also has *conventions* that guide behaviour, including language behaviour. There are social rules controlling who should speak, to whom, for how long, when and where, and in which language. There are social norms for polite and impolite forms of speech; there are taboo words and topics. These social rules are a good indication of power relations as many of them reflect the values of the people or groups in society who have power. This is particularly true when different groups do not have equal language rights. Here is an obvious example. Where teachers have more power than their students, they can call their students what they like. They can use first names or surnames only, or even insulting names that they have made up. Students, however, have to call teachers by their surnames and a title such as *Mr* or *Ms*; some students even have to call their teachers *Sir* or *Mistress* or *Ma'm*.

We forget that these rules of use are social conventions constructed by human beings. It is easier to remember this when we compare the rules of our own speech community with those of a different community. For example, different communities have different rules for who should greet first, a younger or older person. Some communities believe it is rude to look a person in the eye when you speak to them. Other groups believe the opposite. Neither is more natural than the other. Both are conventions. These unwritten rules of use determine what a speech community considers *appropriate* language behaviour. Whose rules win out is a question of power.

I once taught a mature African woman who never spoke unless invited to do so. This was a rule that governed women's speech in her community. The students saw her as a victim of a sexist practice and wanted her to adopt the interaction patterns used at the university and to contribute whenever she had something to say. She refused, and so her peers had to learn to ask her for her opinion. What they discovered when they did this is that if you ask someone to speak, you have to listen to what they say.

In challenging their 'normal' style of classroom interaction, this mature student helped everyone to see that there was nothing natural about it. She led her peers to understand that their assumption that their Anglo practices would determine the nature of the classroom interaction was just as disempowering as the patriarchal practices of her community.

FOOD FOR THOUGHT 1:
WHO IS SPOKEN TO? WHO IS HEARD?

I once went with my family to a game lodge where we were assigned a female ranger to take us out into the bush. She gave my husband and my sons her full attention. She told them stories and encouraged them to tell theirs. My daughter-in-law and I might as well have been in the next room. She no doubt assumed that my husband would be settling the bill. Unluckily for her, I was and so the generous tip she was expecting failed to appear.

FOOD FOR THOUGHT 2:
NAMING

George W. Bush was famous for what analysts have called 'sound bites'—short, compelling ways of naming a situation. Calling his education policy 'No child left behind' was brilliant. It becomes difficult to voice disapproval of any aspect of this policy or its implementation because then it looks as though you want children to be left behind. However, I wonder if George Bush and his supporters understand that his education policy of 'no child left behind' implies 'no child left in front'. I wonder if he would find support for a policy of no child excelling to achieve his or her full potential.

Janks's model for critical literacy

In *Literacy and Power* (Janks 2010), I argue that critical literacy work has to pay attention to questions of *power*, *diversity*, *access* and both *design* and *redesign*, and to recognize their inter-dependence. Because these ideas inform this book, it is important to understand each of these key terms and their relation to language, text and discourse.

Power

The relationship between language and power is not obvious and so the texts and activities in this book attempt to raise awareness of the ways in which language can be used and is used to maintain and to challenge existing forms of power.

There can be little doubt that power matters, both to people who have it and to those who do not. This book will try to show that, because there are connections between language and power, language also matters.

In any *unequal relation of power* there are topdogs and underdogs. How people get to be on top in a society has to do with what that society values. It may be age or maleness or wealth or cleverness, the number of wives one has or the colour of one's skin. It is easier for those who have power to maintain it if they can persuade everyone in the society that there is nothing unnatural about these arrangements, that things are this way because that is the way they are meant to be.

If people *consent* to being powerless then those in power need to use less *force* (armies, police, courts) to maintain their power. Convincing and persuading people to consent to society's rules is often the job of families, religions, schools and the media. All these social institutions use language and it is largely in and through language that meaning is mobilized to keep things the way they are.

It is important to remember that few people are powerful in every sphere of their lives. A CEO of a company might defer to her husband as the head of the house; a favourite child may be bullied at school; a factory worker who has to take orders from his supervisor may be an office bearer in his church. The professor of medicine is vulnerable as a cancer patient.

When thinking about the situations in which they are either topdogs or underdogs, some children in a primary school classroom in Australia decided that often they are neither. They invented the term *middle dogs*.

The either-or topdog–underdog theory of power began with Karl Marx's analysis of social class and the difference in power between owners and workers. But his idea of dominant (bosses/topdog) and subordinate (workers/underdog) groups was soon extended to other forms of oppression such as race, gender, age and ethnicity amongst other social differences.

Language and power

Differences in identity and power affect who has the right to speak and act in different situations as well as who gets heard when they do speak or noticed when they take action. Our attitudes to these differences affect our ideas of whose language is important and whose is not. They affect decisions about whose language is appropriate and inappropriate. They affect people's opportunities and life chances.

But *language is also used to challenge the way things are*. By refusing to consent and by working together people can bring about change. What makes critical literacy *critical* is its concern with the politics of meaning: the ways in which dominant meanings are maintained or challenged and changed.

From the beginning, in the work of Paulo Freire (1972b, p. 61), critical literacy was seen as a means of liberation. If he could teach his adult learners to recognize how their world had been constructed ('named') and if he could help them to see where such naming was oppressive, then they could liberate themselves by renaming their world. For him reading the *word* included reading the *world* in order to change it. Thus social transformation that strives to achieve fairness and equality is at the heart of critical literacy.

Discourse and power

Because our world is constructed in and by language, it shapes our understanding of it together with our sense of self and of others. Edward Said's (1978) analysis of colonial documents shows how ways of talking about the East systematically constructed the West as superior and Oriental people as backward and degenerative (p. 206), irrational (p. 38), primitive (p. 231), and generally inferior to 'white men' (p. 226). This continues into present-day discourses about Islam and its threat to the US and the rest of Western civilization.

More importantly, we grow up unconsciously absorbing the discourses of the people around us. James Gee (1990) defines discourse as the *ways of speaking/writing-doing-being-believing and valuing* of the people around us. These discourses construct identity positions for us and produce us as particular kinds of human subjects. This is language at its most powerful and it is no doubt why Foucault (1970) believes that 'discourse is the power which is to be seized'. It is why people like Ngũgî wa Thiong'o (1991) argue that people who have grown up in discourses that construct them as inferior have to 'decolonize' their minds. As Freire (1972b, p. 61) said, they have to rename themselves and their place in the world.

Diversity

People who grow up in different communities learn different languages and different social and linguistic conventions. They have different rules for interacting, for dressing and for comporting their bodies. They are exposed to different discourses and have different beliefs and values. They read different texts for different purposes and go to schools that privilege different kinds of knowledge. These are just a few of the differences that produce human diversity and variation in our ways of constructing and experiencing the world.

However, people move outside of the communities into which they were born and encounter different ways of being in the world. For some people this creates opportunities to learn additional languages and to consider other beliefs and values. They see difference as productive, as a chance to expand their knowledge and their own horizons of possibility. Many acquire hybrid identities and learn to be comfortable in a number of different discourses.

On the other hand, there are those who experience difference as a threat to their own identities. They construct a divide between *us*, our people, and *them*, the strange and dangerous others. Sometimes these divisions result in

- constructing the Other as inferior (as is the case with racist representations of colonized people)
- excluding the Other, expelling them from the country or making them live in separate areas or ghettos (as was the case with Apartheid in South Africa)
- killing the Other. In extreme cases this results in genocide (as happened during the holocaust in Germany where Hitler set out to exterminate Jews, gypsies and homosexuals).

Difference often results in the construction of hierarchies. One can think of a hierarchy as a ladder with differences arranged on the steps from top to bottom. Languages are a good example of this. If more than one language is spoken in a country then one is usually seen to be the powerful and prestigious language with the others ranked below in relation to their status. People who can speak the language of power fluently and who are highly literate in that language are likely to have more power and influence.

In a similar way people tend to rank different kinds of work. Professional work tends to be valued more highly than manual labour and it is better paid. Then, within the professions, in South Africa, judges and doctors receive more esteem than teachers and nurses. These rankings give people at the top of the ladder more power than people below them.

Access

Access is the third idea that we need to consider for critical literacy. We need to ask questions about who gets the kind of education that is needed for professional qualifications. Who gets access to the language of power and its prestige variety? Who gets access to high-status knowledge?

It is important to ask questions about what knowledge is valued in our societies and whose knowledge this is. Whose version of history is taught in schools, whose music, whose art, whose literature, whose language, whose belief system? Should we Africanize the curriculum in South Africa? Should schools in Arizona teach Mexican-American studies? Should schools teach creationism? Should schools offer bilingual education? These are not trivial questions; they determine what it is that students are or are not given access to.

Children from middle-class backgrounds often find that the knowledge that is valued in their homes is also valued in school, whereas working-class or migrant children find that the funds of knowledge that they have acquired at home are excluded from school. This can affect how different children relate to school and how well they do.

You might like to explore what your school considers to be the knowledge worth knowing and what it leaves out. You might have a discussion about who benefits from these decisions.

It is also important to think about who gets easy access to this high-status school knowledge and who finds access difficult and why. For example, it is hard to become literate if there are very few books or other printed material in the language you speak. This is the situation for most of the African languages in South Africa that are taught in schools. It is harder to learn in an overcrowded classroom where there is one teacher to fifty or sixty students. It is harder to learn in a second or foreign language. It is difficult to get access to the internet if you do not have a computer at home or at school. It is hard to learn if you are cold or hungry.

Michel Foucault's research led him to argue that 'any system of education is a political way of maintaining or modifying . . . [who gets access to which discourses], along with the knowledges and powers that they carry' (1972, p. 123). Others have described education as a 'dividing practice' that separates children into haves and have-nots.

Access is also affected by *how* we are taught and how we learn. Different people have different learning styles, different levels of fluency in the language of the classroom, different aptitudes and abilities, different concentration spans, different interests. It is worth thinking about how you learn and what you need to support your learning. In discussion you can find out what others need and how you can support them. It is also worth talking about whether learning in your school is more co-operative or more competitive and how this affects access for different students.

Design

Design is the word I use for making and shaping texts. The word *write* works for texts made of language, whereas design enables us to talk about how we select and organize the full range of meaning-making signs included in texts: words, layout, images, colour, font, movement, sound, and so forth. The ability to manipulate signs and abstract symbols (language and math) is what gives us the edge in a world where the ability to create knowledge and well-designed products is what produces wealth.

Bill Gates is an example of a man who created new knowledge—the Microsoft operating system and the software that gave us access to home computing. Apple, run by Steve Jobs, overtook

Microsoft because Jobs understood the importance of combining knowledge-making and brilliant design. This has made Apple products (Mac computers, iPods, iPhones and iPads) both highly functional and highly desirable.

From a critical literacy perspective it is important to have control over both text production and the technologies that enable us to produce texts. Why? Because text production enables us to

- choose what meanings to make and in doing so to act on the world
- recognise how we are positioning ourselves and our readers by the choices we make as we write
- gain an understanding of how texts are constructed and the possibilities and constraints of different modes for the making of meaning
- gain the experience we need to redesign our own texts as well as the texts of others.

Redesign

Redesign is an act of transformation. The deconstruction of texts and practices is sterile unless we can see how to reconstruct them so as to improve the way we live and relate to one another. Because not even a redesigned text is neutral, we have to think of reconstruction as an ongoing process of transformation. From a critical literacy perspective, each redesign should contribute to creating a world where power is not used to disempower others, where difference is seen as a resource and where everyone has access to social goods and opportunity.

This can be represented in what I have called the redesign cycle. See Figure 0.1.

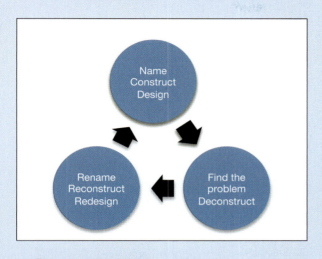

0.1 The redesign cycle
Source: Janks 2010.

Redesigning texts is not a hard thing to imagine or do. Redesigning practices is more of a challenge because ways of doing and acting are often ingrained. Redesigning the world seems like an impossible thing to do.

The important thing to remember is that small changes can make a difference. Planting a tree, recycling garbage, sharing a sandwich, standing up to a bully, fighting for wheelchair ramps, or learning someone else's language may not seem like much, but each in their own way can contribute to making the world a better place for all. If everyone manages to make one small difference a day, to resist practices that disempower them and to speak and act so as not to disempower others, then bit by bit we can contribute to the struggle for human freedom.

FOOD FOR THOUGHT 3:
WHOSE HOME LANGUAGE MATTERS?

Recently in South Africa, I was with Sonia Nieto,[1] a distinguished American scholar. A South African-Israeli, whom we had only just met socially, engaged her in conversation about language issues in the US. Taking her for a white, native speaker of English, he expressed the view that Spanish migrants in the US should not speak Spanish but English. If they live in the US, he told us, they should 'melt', no doubt referring to the metaphor of 'America' as the great 'melting pot' where anyone is supposed to be able to achieve the 'American dream' and become successful.

What he did not know is that Dr Nieto identifies herself as a Puerto Rican-American, her husband comes from Spain and members of her family are Spanish-English bilinguals. She is a qualified bilingual educator, who is known internationally for her work in bilingual and multicultural education.

It was interesting to see this man come face to face with someone who both challenged his taken-for-granted view of language as well as his stereotype of Latinas. What was remarkable about this incident was this man's assumption that perfect strangers would agree with what is obviously the naturalized common sense of the Americans he associates with. I cannot help but wonder whether, as an English-speaking migrant to Israel, he and his family gave up speaking English in their home. If he did not, as I suspect, I wonder how he would explain why he has different standards for Sonia Nieto's family?

Doing Critical Literacy is divided into nine sections. These sections were written by different writers, either alone or with others.

Section 1, written by Hilary Janks, focuses on texts as partial re-presentations of the world and how to read them critically. It is particularly concerned with the positioning of texts and how this relates to questions of *power*.

Sections 2 and 3 work with language, identity and power. *Section 2*, written by Janks, looks at how our identities are shaped by language and discourse and how language sets up identity as the same or different.

Section 3, written by Kerryn Dixon, continues this work with activities that focus our attention on different languages and different varieties (dialects) of the same language. Here identity is affected by which languages we do and do not speak and society's attitudes towards them. Both of these sections work with *diversity* and *Othering* as well as how the languages we speak affect power and *access*.

Sections 4, 5 and 6 provide tools for analysis. *Section 4*, written by Janks, works with word choice and grammar, and emphasizes those aspects of language that are the most useful for *designing* and analyzing texts critically.

Section 5, written by Ana Ferreira and Denise Newfield, works with the tools for visual analysis. But this is also the section that helps you to understand what is meant by critical *visual* literacy. These two sections focus on the *design* of texts and provide an understanding of how texts are constructed and how they can be deconstructed to show how *power* is working through them.

The activities in *Section 6,* written by Dixon, lead to an understanding of how the management of space and time underpins relations of *power*. Space and time are particularly helpful for thinking about how these exercise control over our bodies in different social practices.

Section 7 brings the different ideas together with activities that give you practice in working with everyday texts. The section on advertising and branding was written by Janks. The middle pages on cartoons, comics, magazines, clothing and street signs were written by Ferreira. Stella Granville wrote the section on newspapers. Here students are invited to look at worldly texts to examine their use of language and image (their *design*) and to explore how these texts contribute to maintaining or challenging existing relations of *power*.

Section 8, written by Dixon and Janks, discusses new digital technologies and their effects on the communication landscape. Who has *access* to which technologies and how they are changing our ideas about ownership and privacy are investigated. The notion of digital *identity* is explored.

Section 9, by Janks, concludes the book with a discussion on how one can use critical literacy for *redesigning* texts and practices. The focus is on the kinds of social and literacy action that can contribute to a more just society.

The references used throughout the sections and in the linking commentary are included at the end of the book.

Section 1: Language and position

Representation

The first page of this section introduces an age-old philosophical question: *What is the relationship between things in the world and their representations?* The thing itself can be represented in words or by an image.

What it is important to remember for reading the world critically is that any re-presentation of the world is a version of the world. I use the word *representation* with a hyphen to emphasize that the world presents itself to us, and we present it *again* in the act of re-presentation. The mere act of translating the world into words or pictures requires text-makers to choose which signs to use. A different person might re-present the same thing using quite different signs.

The maps on pages 14 and 15 are examples of texts that re-present the world differently.

Positioning

The versions that texts offer us are *positioned*. What this means is that writers shape texts based on amongst other things

- their beliefs, values and attitudes
- their social positions (age, race, class, ethnicity, etc.)
- how they are positioned relative to the ground (e.g. high up in a football stadium)
- where they are in the world (e.g. country, East or West)
- their experiences (e.g. education, languages, travel, etc.).

The idea of positioning is developed from pages 14–24. It starts with where we are in the world, then moves to where we are standing literally, our position in physical space, and what this enables us to see or not to see (p. 16). On this page it also moves to our positions in the social world. It concludes with an activity on page 17 that shows how a text can position the reader.

Debates usually have two sides to them: a position for an idea or a position against an idea. Debating the topics on page 17 gives practice in taking up a *for* or an *against* position.

Positions of writers and readers

The relationship between the writer's position and the reader's position is explained in a diagram on page 18. Activities on pages 19–25 give you practice in working with these ideas.

Context

Page 23 shows how positioning is tied to context—who is representing what, to whom, when, where, and why? Page 23 then shows how texts are inter-connected and refer to one another. This also affects how texts are positioned and how we read these positions.

The four roles of the reader/writer

To do critical literacy you have to become a particular kind of reader—a text analyst (see page 27). But you cannot do this without also being competent in all four roles of the reader, which are explained on pages 27–28.

Language, power and politics

Page 31 is pivotal. It looks backwards to previous pages and forwards to what is still to come. Because we are concerned with the relationship between language and power, people often assume that this work is about the use of language in national and international politics. Certainly critical literacy will help you to spot spin and to recognize the positions that politicians are constructing for their voters. But critical literacy works with the power relations in everyday life. It is therefore important to understand the distinction between big *P* politics and little *p* politics. It is worth looking back at the texts and activities on pages XX–XX in order to consider which kind of politics they are dealing with.

Pages 28–30 turn more specifically to the relationship between language and power. The old children's rhyme,

> Sticks and stones may break my bones, but words can never harm me

is simply not true. Both words and images can hurt people. They can tease, they can wound, they can belittle, they can insult, they can incite people to violence, they can create and spread hatred, they can be racist, sexist and homophobic, they can do a great deal of damage. That is why critical literacy is interested in seeing how power can work *in* and *through* language.

The texts and activities in this section make you think about language, power and the effects that language and texts can have on and in society. The section concludes with a set of critical questions to ask of texts. These can be applied throughout the book.

Connections between power, diversity, access, design and redesign

How texts are *design*ed and how this affects the positions they offer the reader are fundamental to understanding the relationship between language, image, text and power. *Power* is the main focus of this section. Because positions are not neutral they tend to support the world-views, beliefs, values, actions and languages of some people and not others. Power relations affect how texts are produced and they in turn affect whether power relations are maintained or challenged and changed.

Section 1 therefore starts with activities that explain positioning in order to provide the understanding needed for considering the social effects of texts. The work on positioning is followed by activities that deal with the social impact of texts. The effects of texts relate to issues of identity and difference, *diversity* and *access*—Who gets access to what? Who is included and who is excluded? Who wins and who loses?

Notice how the word de*sign* includes the word *sign*. A design is a selection and arrangement of verbal, visual and other signs. If a design is simply a version of the world, then signs can be re-arranged to provide alternative versions. A number of texts and activities in this section, on pages 14–15, 21, 22, 24–25 either use redesigned texts or invite you to redesign a text.

THINGS—WORDS ABOUT THINGS—IMAGES OF THINGS

Looking at things and recreating them in words and pictures

- Place a chair in front of the blackboard.
- Write the word for 'chair' in all the languages that the class knows on the board.
- Draw an image of the chair on the board.
- Write a definition of a chair on the board. You can make one up or copy one out of a dictionary.

Individual writing activity
Write a description of the chair.

Questions to discuss in groups
1. Which is the real chair?
2. What is the relationship between the words for 'chair' and the chair?
3. What is the relationship between the drawing and the chair?
4. What is the difference between the definition of the chair and the description?
5. What is the relationship between the chair and its definition and the chair and its description?
6. Compare your descriptions. Notice how each description provides a different version of the chair.

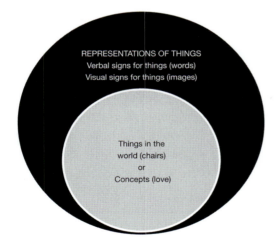

REPRESENTATION

Signs re-present things to us in words or pictures. They stand in for the things themselves.

Signs are abstract representations of things—signs are made up ways of re-presenting the world.

FIGURE 1.1 Things and representations of things

Google Joseph Kusoth's artwork called *One and Three Chairs*. Kusoth provides us with a way of understanding that all texts are representations of the world. His work is the inspiration for this activity.

EAST IS EAST AND WEST IS WEST, OR IS IT?

1. Where do we have to be standing in the world for the 'Middle East' to be in the middle and in the east?
2. Where do we have to be standing in the world for Japan to be in the 'Far East' and the 'West Indies' to be in the west at the same time?
3. If we are in China, where is America?
4. According to this map what is at the centre of the world? Where are the margins? Who lives on the periphery?
5. Who do you think called Australia 'Down under'?
6. Who do you think drew the maps? Why did they draw them this way? Does anyone benefit from this representation of the world? Is anyone disadvantaged?

This map of the world, without the Antarctic, is what we are used to. It has come to be accepted as natural as a result of social convention.

Greenland: 0.8 mil sq miles

GREEN LAND

AFRICA

Africa: 11.6 mil sq miles

FIGURE 1.2

NORTH IS UP AND SOUTH IS DOWN BUT THE WORLD IS ROUND

7. Now, who is on top of the world?
8. Does this map make you see the world differently? How does this make you feel?
9. Is this map wrong?
10. Does the world have a top and a bottom? What if you see it from outer space?
11. What do the maps of Africa below tell you about maps as representations?

This map challenges our conventional views of North–South relations.

Africa: 11.6 mil sq miles

AFRICA

GREEN LAND

FIGURE 1.3   Greenland: 0.8 mil sq miles

Find the FIFA world cup poster with the face of a woman in the shape of the map of Africa. See www.fifa.com/mm/StaticPhoto/world cup/organisation/emblems posters/poster/2010_poster.jpg.

FIGURE 1.4

FIGURE 1.5

MAPS ARE TEXTS—TEXTS ARE REPRESENTATIONS

1. What is the difference between the next two maps? Which is more accurate?

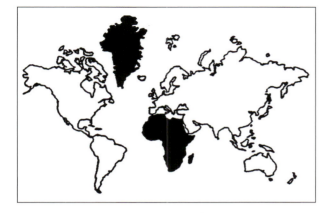

This map is known as the Mercator projection. It is the representation that is most familiar to us. This map maintains the shape of the continents but distorts their size.

FIGURE 1.6

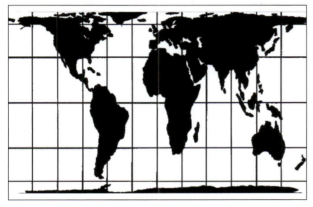

This map, known as the Peters projection, first appeared in 1974. This map maintains the relative size of the continents but distorts their shapes.

FIGURE 1.7

The earth is round. The challenge of any world map is to represent a round earth on a flat surface. . . . The Mercator projection creates increasing distortions of size as you move away from the equator. Mapmakers call this 'the Greenland Problem' because Greenland appears to be the same size as Africa, yet Africa is fourteen times larger. Because the Mercator distortion is worst at the poles it is common to leave Antarctica off the map. This results in the Northern Hemisphere appearing much larger than it really is. The equator appears about 60% of the way down the map, diminishing the size and importance of the developing countries (see www.diversophy.com/petersmap.htm).

2. The Peters projection created a great deal of controversy when it was first published. Why do you think this was so? What do you think people argued about? Who would lose if Peters' map was recognized? Who stood to gain? Why?

Hmm. . . .
Two maps.
More than one valid
point of view. . . .
HmmHmm.

WHERE WE STAND AFFECTS WHAT WE 'SEE'

FIGURE 1.8   The blind men and the elephant
By John Godfrey Saxe (1816-1887)

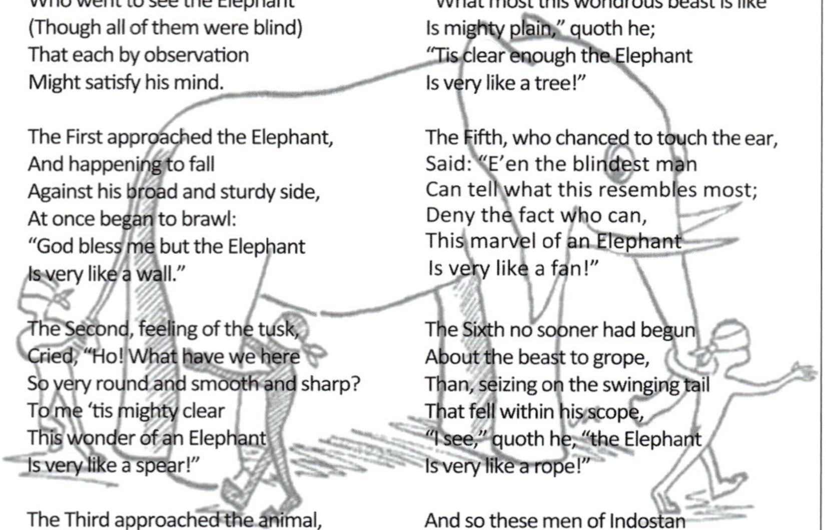

It was six men of Indostan
To learning much inclined,
Who went to see the Elephant
(Though all of them were blind)
That each by observation
Might satisfy his mind.

The First approached the Elephant,
And happening to fall
Against his broad and sturdy side,
At once began to brawl:
"God bless me but the Elephant
Is very like a wall."

The Second, feeling of the tusk,
Cried, "Ho! What have we here
So very round and smooth and sharp?
To me 'tis mighty clear
This wonder of an Elephant
Is very like a spear!"

The Third approached the animal,
And happening to take
The squirming trunk within his hands,
Thus boldly up and spake:
"I see," quoth he, "The Elephant
Is very like a snake!"

The Fourth reached out an eager hand,
And felt around the knee,
"What most this wondrous beast is like
Is mighty plain," quoth he;
"Tis clear enough the Elephant
Is very like a tree!"

The Fifth, who chanced to touch the ear,
Said: "E'en the blindest man
Can tell what this resembles most;
Deny the fact who can,
This marvel of an Elephant
Is very like a fan!"

The Sixth no sooner had begun
About the beast to grope,
Than, seizing on the swinging tail
That fell within his scope,
"I see," quoth he; "the Elephant
Is very like a rope!"

And so these men of Indostan
Disputed loud and long,
Each of his own opinion
Exceeding stiff and strong,
Though each was partly in the right,
And all were in the wrong!

Each man's impression of an elephant is based on where he happens to be standing in relation to it.[2]

WHAT WE SEE AFFECTS HOW WE RE-PRESENT EVENTS

Say how what can be seen is affected by

- where you are sitting at a football match
- where the teacher is standing in class
- where you are sitting at break or recess
- where you are dancing in a crowded party.

Can you imagine other situations such as these? How does what you can see affect the way you tell someone about these events? Another way of asking this question is to ask '*How is your account positioned?*'

OUR SOCIAL POSITIONS AFFECT OUR POINTS OF VIEW

So far we have seen how our actual *position* in physical space affects what we can see. We have also considered how what we can see affects how we re-present things. Maps show us that geographical location or *position* affects how people see the world and how they map it. It is not surprising that early European mapmakers *positioned* Europe at the centre of their maps. Now we need to think about how our social positions—as men or women, young or old, rich or poor— affect our points of view. Make a list of other social positions that are likely to affect our standpoints on issues in our lives.

1. Give examples of issues on which people are likely to disagree because of their gender.
2. Give examples of issues on which you and your parents are likely to disagree because of age.
3. How might teachers' and students' views on homework differ?
4. How might people's standpoint on English's status as a global language be affected by the languages that they speak?

You probably noticed that in your groups not all the young women agreed with one another and the same for the young men. One of the reasons for this is that we are not *just* female or *just* male. We are also young or old, middle class or working class, religious or not religious. All the different positions that we occupy also influence what we think and believe. As a result we find differences *within* gender groups. What this suggests is that social positioning influences our views but it does not determine them.

POSITIONING

The next passage shows clearly how the writer constructs a position for himself or herself as well as a position for the reader. The passage constructs both the writer and the reader.

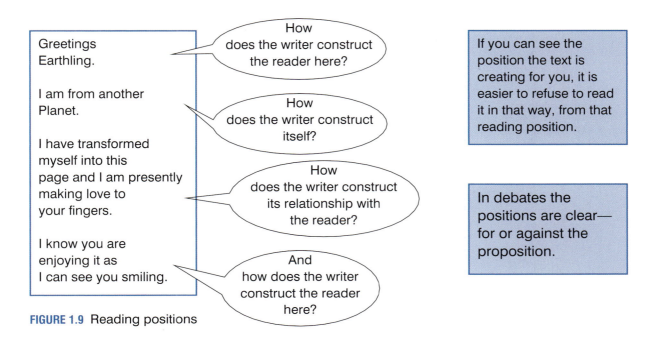

Greetings Earthling.

I am from another Planet.

I have transformed myself into this page and I am presently making love to your fingers.

I know you are enjoying it as I can see you smiling.

How does the writer construct the reader here?

How does the writer construct itself?

How does the writer construct its relationship with the reader?

And how does the writer construct the reader here?

FIGURE 1.9 Reading positions

If you can see the position the text is creating for you, it is easier to refuse to read it in that way, from that reading position.

In debates the positions are clear— for or against the proposition.

FIGURE 1.10 Alien

Choose one of the following debate topics. In groups work out arguments for and against the propositions and then conduct the debate according to the rules for debating.[3]

- It is unethical to clone human beings.
- The job of schools is to create productive and disciplined workers.
- The State has a right to make corporal punishment in the home illegal.
- Wearing any markers of a religious faith should not be allowed in schools.

THE WRITER, THE READER AND THE TEXT ARE ALL POSITIONED

How we see the world—our point of view—affects the way we present this world to other people. Where we stand, literally, socially and ideologically, shapes the way we construct texts and the way in which we read texts.

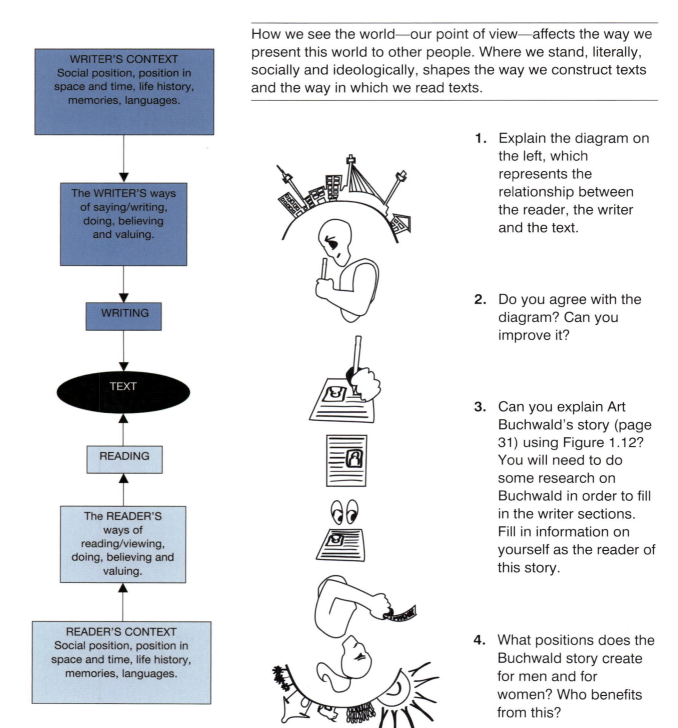

WRITER'S CONTEXT
Social position, position in space and time, life history, memories, languages.

The WRITER'S ways of saying/writing, doing, believing and valuing.

WRITING

TEXT

READING

The READER'S ways of reading/viewing, doing, believing and valuing.

READER'S CONTEXT
Social position, position in space and time, life history, memories, languages.

FIGURE 1.11
Writer, text, and reader
Based on Jones, 1990 and Gee, 1990.

FIGURE 1.12
Writer, text, and reader
Illustration by Daniel Janks.

1. Explain the diagram on the left, which represents the relationship between the reader, the writer and the text.

2. Do you agree with the diagram? Can you improve it?

3. Can you explain Art Buchwald's story (page 31) using Figure 1.12? You will need to do some research on Buchwald in order to fill in the writer sections. Fill in information on yourself as the reader of this story.

4. What positions does the Buchwald story create for men and for women? Who benefits from this?

THE SPEAKER'S OR WRITER'S POSITION AND THE READER'S POSITION

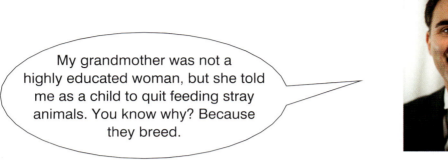

FIGURE 1.13 André Bauer, the lieutenant governor of South Carolina

My grandmother was not a highly educated woman, but she told me as a child to quit feeding stray animals. You know why? Because they breed.

1. How does Bauer construct a position for his grandmother? Why does he do this?
2. What is Bauer's grandmother's position on stray animals?
3. Does Bauer agree with his grandmother? How do you know?
4. Do you agree with Bauer and his grandmother?

If, when you read what Bauer said, you
- agree with what he said, then you are the *ideal reader* who is reading *with* the text
- disagree with what he said, then you are a *resistant reader* who is reading *against* the text.

If we place this quote in context, the story gets more interesting. According to *Time* (Verbatim, 8 February 2010), Bauer said this when he was 'criticizing policies that extend welfare benefits to the poor'.

5. How does Bauer use language to position poor people?
6. Do you agree with his position on welfare?
7. Why is an understanding of context important?

When we listen to, read or view texts, it is important to *engage* with them. As critical readers we need to work out what the text is saying and to think about that in relation to our own beliefs and values.

But we also have to step back from the text to ask critical questions.

What positions is the writer constructing? What does he or she want us to think? Who is the *ideal reader*? What is the ideal reading position? Then we have to ask ourselves whose interests are being served. Who benefits? Who does not? If we do this we become *resistant readers* who do not blindly buy into the meanings and positions that texts offer us.

THE CHOICES MADE BY TEXT PRODUCERS CREATE POSITIONS

> It is not possible to produce a text without making choices. Designers of texts have to choose from a range of possible options. These are choices of what to say as well as how to say it.

Role play—refusing a date

1. Work in same-gender groups of three to five. Imagine that you do not wish to accept an invitation to go on a date. List ten different ways of saying 'no'.

   > 'No' is the *what* of the message and the ten different ways are the *how*.

2. Role play this situation in same-gender or cross-gender pairs. In each pair there is an asker and a refuser. As soon as you begin to act, you are also making decisions about tone of voice, eye contact and body language in addition to decisions about language. These are also part of the *how* and they affect the meaning of the message.

3. Now look at the different choices made for each refusal. Try to work out how each refusal constructs a position for the person asking for the date. Because that asker can choose or refuse to be constructed by the refusal, it is important to see how he or she reacts to being turned down. You should expect to see a connection between the form of the rejection (the how) and the reaction to it.

> Every choice positions the speaker, the writer, the listener or the reader and the text differently. Because we make choices, texts are not neutral. They are selective.

Discuss the postcards and the cartoon below.

FIGURE 1.14   FIGURE 1.15   FIGURE 1.16

DIFFERENT VERBAL CHOICES HAVE DIFFERENT EFFECTS

Text A has been adapted from 'Lighting up with Lit', an article in the *Sunday Times*, 14 March 2010, p.14, by Kate Sidley. Text A was then redesigned to create Text B. Neither of these texts is neutral.

1. Compare texts A and B and decide how their differences create different positions for sport, reading and music, as well as for the students, the teachers and the parents.

Text A	Text B
The school hierarchy deifies the boy who can find the corner of the net or the girl with the glorious backstroke. Even musicians get their share of the limelight, with performances where their parents can bask in the glow of their offspring's achievements. But what if your child is really really good at reading? No one schlepps across town to watch her read. The school does not provide tasty teas at half time. Dad doesn't run up and down the sidelines risking a coronary. That is until Wayne Mills began to promote the 'sport of reading'. Now Kids' Lit Quizzes are held as far afield as China and parents are there smiling and punching the air.	Since Wayne Mills' Kid Lit Quizzes made reading too cool for school, ten out of ten on a quiz is the bookish equivalent of hitting a home run. Now kids who are really really good at reading can share the limelight. Before this, principals, teachers and parents treated the students who are brilliant at sport like gods and they attended matches to bask in the glory of their triumphs. Being sporty eclipsed being bookish. Even musicians got to perform and be at the centre of the stage. Not any more. Now Wayne Mills' quizzes are held as far afield as China and bookworms are receiving the fame and recognition previously reserved for jocks.

TABLE 1.1 Different text positions

2. Try to rewrite Text A as neutrally as you can.

3. Compare your text with a partner's. Notice how choices of words and of sequence affect meaning, so that no text is un-positioned.

4   Now draw or find pictures (in magazines or on the net) of students who are good at sport and students who are good at reading. Discuss the different representations.

5   How do the pictures alongside construct the sporty person and the bookish person?

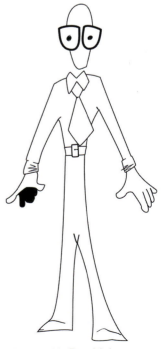

FIGURE 1.17 Sporty person

FIGURE 1.18 Bookish person

DIFFERENT VISUAL CHOICES HAVE DIFFERENT EFFECTS

How do the visual choices made for each of these collages create a different identity for each of the designers shown in the image? Now make a collage to design your own identity so as to attract a potential date.

FIGURE 1.19 Design Indaba poster

POSITIONING OCCURS IN CONTEXTS

We have seen how where we are in space and how we are located socially affects both how we produce texts and how we interpret them. WHERE is part of the context. We also need to know who is saying what to whom, when, where and why.

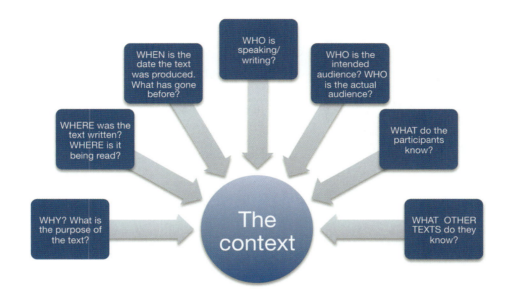

FIGURE 1.20

Words have meaning in contexts so we need knowledge of the context to understand how positioning is working.

FIGURE 1.21

Source: www.war-stories.com/aspprotect/images/poster-wwi-ally-england-your-country-needs-you.jpg.

Have you seen this poster before? What period in history does it come from?

What could you guess about the purpose of this text from the choice of words and image?

Now do some research so as to answer the questions WHO, WHERE, WHAT, WHEN and WHY set out above.

Do the image and the words make readers feel as if the poster is speaking directly to them? If so, how? If not, why not?

How does this poster affect your reading of the Colman's mustard advertisement?

Section 1: Language and position

WHAT WE KNOW FROM PREVIOUS TEXTS IS PART OF THE CONTEXT

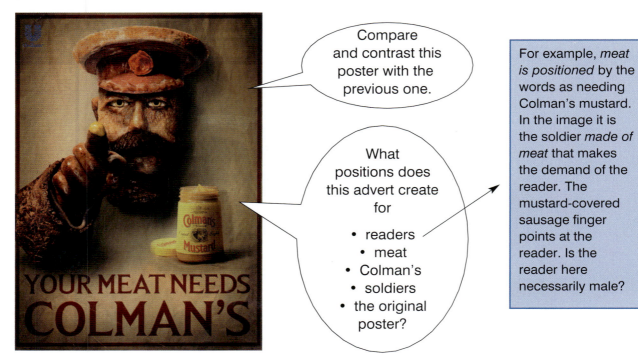

Compare and contrast this poster with the previous one.

What positions does this advert create for

- readers
- meat
- Colman's
- soldiers
- the original poster?

For example, *meat is positioned* by the words as needing Colman's mustard. In the image it is the soldier *made of meat* that makes the demand of the reader. The mustard-covered sausage finger points at the reader. Is the reader here necessarily male?

FIGURE 1.22

Figures 1.23 and 1.24 are cigarette advertisements from the 1950s. Explain how the passing of time has changed the position of the reader. Compare them with more recent adverts on Google Images.

Texts interact and affect one another. The meaning of any text is affected by other related texts.

This is known as INTERTEXTUALITY.

FIGURE 1.23   **FIGURE 1.24**

THE MEANINGS AND THE SOCIAL EFFECTS OF TEXTS

This image of President Obama appeared in *Time*, Volume 175, No. 4, 1 February 2010.

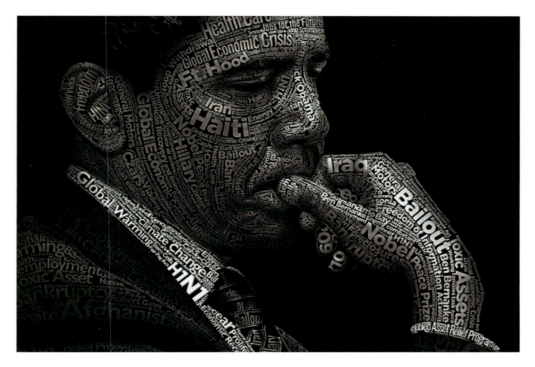

FIGURE 1.25 President Obama

Source: illustration for *Time* by Dylan Roscover.

What meanings can you find in this text? What words and what visual elements create these meanings?

- What effects might this text have? On Obama? On his advisers? On his opponents? On his supporters? On his family? On ordinary citizens of the United States? On the economy?

- Write a caption for this picture that shows you are on his side.

- Write a caption for this picture that shows you are not on his side.

- Compare your captions with those of your fellow students.

- When you have completed this activity, consider the caption that appeared in *Time* and decide whether *Time* is sympathetic to Obama or not.[4]

- Compare this image with other more upbeat images of Obama.

> Another way of talking about taking sides is to say that some texts are *positioned* in support of Obama and some texts are *positioned* against him. Different texts are differently *positioned*.

THE FOUR ROLES OF THE READER

Text decoder

Readers of English have to recognize the letters of the alphabet and know what sounds they stand for. They have to know how these sounds combine to make words, and how words make sentences.

Chinese does not have letters; it has characters. Each character represents one idea or concept. To read Chinese writing one has to recognize the idea encoded by each character and one has to be able to recognize 3,000 to 4,000 characters to be functionally literate.

Readers of images have to look at all their different elements—the shots, the framing, the subject matter, the composition, the colour, etc. in order to see what is there and how these choices combine to make meaning.

Decoders can crack the text's code. They can read it silently or aloud.

FIGURE 1.26 Text decoder

Text participant

Text participants have to interact with the text. They have to take meaning from the text and bring meaning to the text.

1. Taking meaning from the text
Participants have to work out what the text is saying and what it means. This is sometimes called comprehension.

2. Bringing meaning to the text
Participants have to think about what the text is saying in relation to what they know and believe. They have to bring their own meanings to the text in order to think about whether they agree with the text or not.

Participants are engaged and active readers. They ask questions. They underline, highlight and annotate texts. They summarize the key ideas or they become involved in the story.

FIGURE 1.27 Text participant

THE FOUR ROLES OF THE READER

Work out the four roles of the WRITER and do your own drawings of these four roles.

FIGURE 1.28

Text user

Text users use texts a lot. They read, write and view all sorts of texts for all sorts of purposes—they read love letters and cereal boxes and web-sites and text books. They read recipe books and newspapers and poetry. They read novels and magazines and SMS messages.

Text users understand that different kinds of texts are used for different social purposes. Because they are familiar with different texts from using them, they can recognize different *genres* (kinds) of texts: advertisements, news reports, instructions, stories, academic journal articles, text messages.

They understand that genres shape the content, form and language of these different kinds of texts that are used for different social purposes.

Text users engage with a variety of texts regularly and frequently and so become familiar with their shape and form.

FIGURE 1.29

(Adapted from Freebody and Luke 1990. Illustrations by Daniel Janks.)

Text analyst

Text analysts pay attention to the social effects of texts.

Analysts pay attention to how texts shape our identities, our society, our beliefs and our values. They recognize that texts are not neutral—texts are constructed by their writers and designers to have particular effects.

Analysts examine the writer's choices to see whose side the text producer is on and to work out who benefits as a result. Who is included? Who is excluded? Who is favoured and who is not? What is present and what is absent? What is shown as natural and inevitable? What is shown as social, that is, as the result of human action?

Analysts try to understand the power relations that are at work in everyday texts. They want to know whose interests are served by the text.

THE MEANINGS AND THE SOCIAL EFFECTS OF TEXTS

Text participant questions about meaning

1.
Describe the rough children in your own words.
2.
Why did the narrator fear them?
3.
Why do you think the parents kept the narrator from these children?
4.
Find all the negative words to describe the rough boys.
5.
What is attractive in the description of the rough boys?
6.
Why does the narrator long to forgive them?
7.
Describe the narrator from the clues in the poem.
8.
What clues can you find as to who these rough boys are?

My parents kept me from children who were rough
by Stephen Spender

My parents kept me from children who were
    rough
and who threw words like stones and who
    wore torn clothes.
Their thighs showed through rags. They ran
    in the street
And climbed cliffs and stripped by the
    country streams.

I feared more than tigers their muscles like
    iron
And their jerking hands and their knees tight
    on my arms.
I feared the salt coarse pointing of those
    boys
Who copied my lisp behind me on the road.

They were lithe, they sprang out behind
    hedges
Like dogs to bark at our world. They threw
    mud
And I looked another way, pretending to
    smile,
I longed to forgive them, yet they never
    smiled.

The image

Who are the rough boys? What stereotypes do the image reinforce? What are the social effects of the image?

Text analyst questions about social effects

9.
According to the poem what kinds of things do boys do? How is masculinity portrayed? What are the consequences for girls who like to climb trees and for boys who like to write poetry?

10.
Could the poem be about the differences between rich and poor boys from different social classes? What are the implications? Whose side does the poet take?
11.
Do you think the narrator is a boy or a girl? Why? Does it matter? Why?
12.
Does this poem reinforce or challenge stereotypes of gender and class?

FIGURE 1.30 Illustration in a South African textbook (1998)

HOW POWER WORKS IN TEXTS

Operation	How the operation works	Examples
Legitimate Represent something as legitimate or worthy of support	• By giving reasons and making a logical argument. • By using tradition. • By telling small stories such as jokes or anecdotes. • By using grand stories like the Bible or the Constitution.	• English is a powerful global language. Powerful languages give people access. Therefore people should learn English. • The tradition of initiation in schools is used as a justification for bullying. • Often people use jokes as a licence for stories that repeat offensive stereotypes. • People use the Bible selectively—Leviticus 18:22—to justify homophobia.
Conceal Disguise or hide the working of power	• By hiding some of the information and telling only half-truths. • By hiding unpleasant realities with the use of euphemism. • Using figures of speech to disguise a situation or present it in a particular light.	• Half-truth: you tell your parents that your brother did not do something and you do not tell them that you offered to do it instead of him. • Euphemisms: 'collateral damage' for the killing of innocent civilians in a bombing raid. 'Ethnic cleansing' for genocide. Describing a soldier as 'Rambo'.
Unify Bring people together to create powerful groups	• By creating an idea (e.g. a nation, a people) that draws people into a group that has a collective identity. • By creating symbols of unity (flags, songs, mottos, uniforms). • The use of standardization (e.g. of a language)	• Under Apartheid the national motto was 'Unity is Strength'. This of course referred to white unity. Other countries have other ways of creating a national identity. • National language policies and the standardization of particular language varieties is an attempt to create unity by making people speak the same language.
Fragment Separate people to divide and rule	• By emphasizing the differences between people in order to split them into different groups. • By constructing an 'us' and a 'them' where 'they' are represented as the dangerous enemy who threatens 'us' and must be wiped out.	• Racial and ethnic segregation under Apartheid is an excellent example of separation that enabled white domination. • Constructing Jews and gypsies and homosexuals as the dangerous Other led to the Holocaust in which 6 million people were exterminated.
'Thingify' Turn actions into things or states of affairs	• By using nouns instead of verbs (e.g. the 'recommendation' instead of 'the authorities recommend'). Nouns have no actors who have to account for their actions. • By using verbs in the passive that delete agents. • By making something seem natural and inevitable—part of nature rather than history. You cannot argue with nature (e.g. the tides just are).	• Decisions about segregation have been implemented. Nouns: decision and segregation. Who decided? What will be segregated and who will do the segregating? • Passive: has been implemented (by whom?). • Because women give birth to babies and have breasts to feed them (nature) they are constructed as naturally more suited to being care-givers and home makers, as in the Buchwald story.

TABLE 1.2 How operations of ideology work in texts

Source: based on Thompson 1990.

RE-ANALYSING A TEXT

Table 1.2 provides a helpful framework for thinking about how power works in texts by describing five operations. The table gives a summary of these together with examples that help you to understand them. While it is good to keep these together in one framework, it is probably best to think about them one at a time and to look for your own examples in newspapers, magazines and this book, bit by bit.

Here we revisit 'My parents kept me from children who were rough' and use Thompson's operations to deepen our understanding of how power is working in this poem. See if this way of interrogating the text helps you to see it differently.

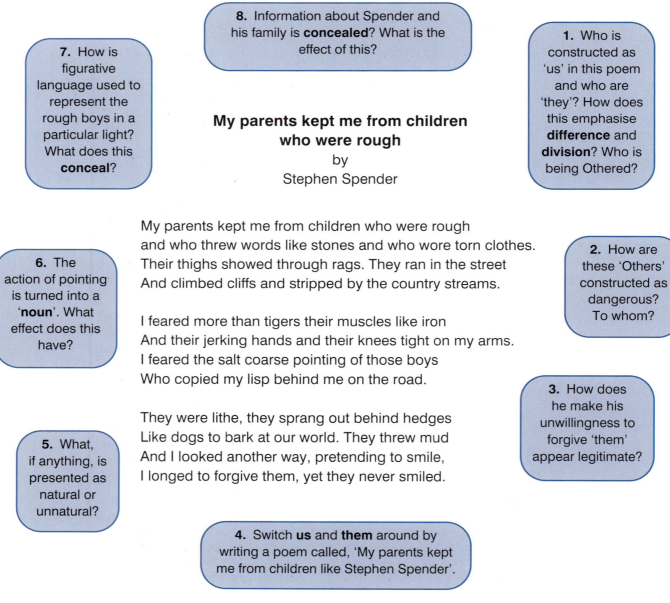

8. Information about Spender and his family is **concealed**? What is the effect of this?

7. How is figurative language used to represent the rough boys in a particular light? What does this **conceal**?

1. Who is constructed as 'us' in this poem and who are 'they'? How does this emphasise **difference** and **division**? Who is being Othered?

My parents kept me from children who were rough

by
Stephen Spender

My parents kept me from children who were rough
and who threw words like stones and who wore torn clothes.
Their thighs showed through rags. They ran in the street
And climbed cliffs and stripped by the country streams.

I feared more than tigers their muscles like iron
And their jerking hands and their knees tight on my arms.
I feared the salt coarse pointing of those boys
Who copied my lisp behind me on the road.

They were lithe, they sprang out behind hedges
Like dogs to bark at our world. They threw mud
And I looked another way, pretending to smile,
I longed to forgive them, yet they never smiled.

6. The action of pointing is turned into a '**noun**'. What effect does this have?

5. What, if anything, is presented as natural or unnatural?

2. How are these 'Others' constructed as dangerous? To whom?

3. How does he make his unwillingness to forgive 'them' appear legitimate?

4. Switch **us** and **them** around by writing a poem called, 'My parents kept me from children like Stephen Spender'.

FIGURE 1.31 Spender revisited

CRITICAL LITERACY AND POLITICS

6. Do you find this story funny?

5. What stereotypes does this story reinforce? Who benefits?

1. What decisions does the wife make? Who makes this kind of decision in your family?

Art Buchwald, a writer and satirist for the *Washington Post*, was asked to give his recipe for a successful marriage, when he was interviewed on his fiftieth wedding anniversary. He claimed that his marriage had worked because his wife made all the small decisions and he made all the big decisions. When asked to give examples of the small decisions his wife made, he said that she decided where they would live, where the children would go to school, who their friends would be, where they should spend their holidays, what they should buy, what he should wear and so forth. 'If these are the small decisions, what then are the big decisions that you make?' asked the interviewer. Buchwald said that he decided all the important things, such as what shares to buy, who should be president of the United States, what should be done about the economy and whether or not the United States should go to war.

4. Who do you think has more control over the outcome of their decisions?

2. What does the husband decide?

3. Do you agree with the definitions of what counts as *big* and what counts as *small*? Why? Why not?

'Politics with a capital *P* is the big stuff, the worldly concerns of the husband.
. . . Little *p* politics, on the other hand, is about the micro-politics of everyday life. It is about the minute-by-minute choices and decisions that make us who we are' (Janks 2010, p. 188).

7. Why are both of these important for critical literacy? Is one more important than the other?

CRITICAL QUESTIONS FOR READERS TO ASK

Text analysts are interested in how the text has been put together and how this relates to power. Power can be thought of as little *p* politics or big *P* politics. Politics in this sense can be defined as power relations in different areas of life.

We have seen how verbal (words) and visual (images) modes are used to produce meaning in texts. Other modes include all the ways that people make meaning: using language, designing images, moving and dressing their bodies, creating music and sounds, organizing space and time. In critical literacy we are particularly interested in how different modes work together in texts and who benefits.

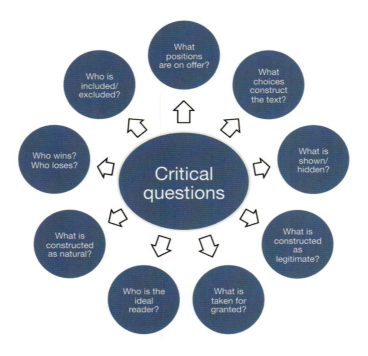

FIGURE 1.32

1. Can you think of other questions to ask to understand how power is working IN texts?

2. Can you think of other questions to ask to understand how power is working THROUGH texts, that is, how the text itself contributes to maintaining or challenging power?

3. Add to this set of questions as you continue working through this book.

Section 2: Identity and diversity

The positive use of language

The main focus of Section 2 is identity and difference. It is specific differences that create human diversity. I use difference and diversity interchangeably.

It starts by recognizing that power can also be used to create positive effects (p. 35). Whereas before we looked at how language can be used to hurt and disempower people, here we recognize that language can also be used to encourage, to praise, to give support or advice, to show love and to speak out against injustice. What matters is how language is used and how power is used.

Identity positions

Pages 36 to 39 extend the idea of positioning in order to explain identity. Texts construct identity positions for readers to take up or not. Discourses also construct identity positions for members of a discourse community. Michel Foucault calls identity positions *subject positions.* As we saw in the main introduction, he sees language and discourse as powerful because of the ways in which they shape our *identities*. The activities on these three pages invite you to think about the ways in which your own identity has been shaped. If you compare the way your identity has been formed with that of your friends, you will find both similarities and differences. Identity and diversity are part of our lives.

Getting you to work with your own different identity positions will help you to recognize the different discourse communities that you belong to (school, work, church, home, music, etc.) (p. 39). It is because we belong to a range of discourse communities that our identities are not limited to the primary discourses of our family and its wider community. Belonging to multiple discourse communities unsettles what we take for granted and this enables us to learn and to change. This can be uncomfortable, especially if the beliefs and values of our own different identity positions are in conflict (pp. 40–41). Page 42 invites you to consider a dispute resulting from conflicting discourses.

Belonging

Part of what it means to belong to a discourse community is to abide by its norms—what it considers appropriate behaviour. If you stray too far from these, you might feel like an outsider or even be excluded. Yet many people in the modern world have hybrid identities. They are bicultural, multilingual and are comfortable with difference.

Othering

Nevertheless, there are people who fear difference. Those who exploit this fear use language to dehumanize The Other and to set *them* up as dangerous and a threat to *us.* This can result in genocide, defined in international law as 'acts committed with intent to destroy, in whole or in part, a national, ethnic, racial or religious group'. Genocide is at the extreme end of emphasizing the differences between people, but it is important to remember that dehumanizing starts in small ways. We can all learn to spot prejudice, racism, grievance, intolerance, aggression, injustice and oppression, and we can try to stop them before they get out of control.

The activities on page 41 invite you to think about why people need a sense of belonging. Page 42 looks at how languages and their varieties work to include some and to exclude others. It then moves on to Othering and suggests that you investigate how dehumanization can work to enable crimes against humanity (pp. 43–45). It then takes the xenophobic attacks in South Africa (p. 46) as a case study in order to show how negative attitudes to others are produced in language and discourse. Despite the fact that all of this is 'no laughing matter', satire is used to help you understand how discourse works (p. 47) and Hollywood movies are explored as a way of understanding *us* and *them* constructions (p. 43). The consideration of difference concludes with a consideration of: who decides what is normal or natural (p. 44); who decides what is abnormal (p. 45); how normality and abnormality are constructed; and who benefits.

Language and the politics of difference

What the section has shown so far is that difference is political. What this means is that we tend to rank differences by constructing some as better than others. Ranking creates inequality: differences in status and power as well as differences in access to education and other kinds of opportunity. Page 48 looks at identities that make people powerful and those that do not and page 49 tells a story in which a young person is treated badly by an adult. It asks you to come up with concrete things that you could do to intervene in the situation. It provides an example of spotting and stopping injustice to others that we encounter in our daily lives.

Pastor Niemöller's (1892–1984) famous quotation about the inactivity of German intellectuals following the Nazi rise to power and the purging of their chosen targets has given people enormous courage to defend human rights.

> First they came for the communists,
> and I didn't speak out because I wasn't a
>   communist.
> Then they came for the trade unionists,
> and I didn't speak out because I wasn't a
>   trade unionist.
> Then they came for the Jews,
> and I didn't speak out because I wasn't a
>   Jew.
> Then they came for me
> and there was no one left to speak out for
>   me.

Notice how in this quotation Niemöller focuses on group identities and not on individual identities. The last pages of this section focus on four options that individuals have if they belong to an oppressed group. They can decide to leave the group (p. 50); they can reconstruct or rename the group positively (p. 51); they can change other uses of language that affect the group (p. 52); they can fight for equality and social transformation (p. 52). The activities work with both big *P* politics (liberation and gay rights movements) and small *p* politics (who gets a turn to speak; whose language is used).

Connections between power, diversity, access, design and redesign

The main focus of Section 2 is on identity and difference and the ways in which language is used to construct them. It works with categories of us and them, belonging and exclusion, as well as construction of the Other. These connect diversity to differences in power and differences in access (to, amongst others, groups, spaces and opportunities). Thompson's operations of unifying and separating (p. 29) lie at the heart of identity constructions. Possibilities for redesign are rooted in language and social action.

BAD POWER AND GOOD POWER

> When power is used to benefit some and to disadvantage others it produces an unjust society with topdogs who have power over underdogs. But power can also be used positively, to free people or to share the planet's resources fairly.

- Give as many examples as you can of people who have used power positively to make people's lives better. These could be people who work on a grand scale, with big *P* politics, to bring about peace or to prevent the collapse of the world's banks. Or they could be people who work on a smaller scale, with little *p* politics, to prevent bullying or to make sure that buildings are accessible to people in wheelchairs or that there is food for vegetarians to eat.

- Then give examples of people in *your* life who have had a good influence on you. What did they do to shape you? Why did you take on the IDENTITY POSITIONS that they offered or suggested? Explain how they used their power in relation to you in a good way.

POWER MAKES US WHO WE ARE

> When we think of texts as creating positions for readers to take up, we should not assume that all these positions are bad. Texts can also teach us to value difference and diversity, to respect our parents, to value education. Foucault is a theorist who sees power as 'productive' because it works to 'produce' us as particular kinds of human beings—as particular kinds of human subjects.

FIGURE 2.1 The wisdom of Spider-Man

Parents are expected to use their power to produce responsible and caring adults. Teachers are expected to use their power to produce educated citizens. According to James Gee, at the same time as we are learning ways of being, we are also learning ways of doing, believing and valuing that are bound up with our ways of speaking and writing, reading and listening. The languages we speak and the ways in which we speak them are also fundamentally linked to our identities.

IDENTITY POSITIONS

We all occupy many different identity or subject positions. We are located differently in relation to social categories such as race, gender, social class, age, sexuality, nationality and ethnicity. We are also born into communities with different religions and languages, and different ways of doing, being and valuing. As we move through life we also take on, or are given, different social roles such as daughter, oldest son, student, husband, mother, grandfather, friend and so forth. Identity is multiple and who we are is shaped by the different groups and communities that we move through during our lives.

At times the shaping feels like deeply ingrained chiselling, at others like gentle moulding. Sometimes we resist. Sometimes we submit. And sometimes we do not even know that it is happening. At times the little instructions, how to sit quietly, stand up straight, face the front and be quiet, discipline our bodies and our behaviour.

> Suggest other metaphors for shaping identities.

Read the poem by Michael Rosen

Chivvy

Grown ups say things like
Speak up
Don't talk with your mouth full
Don't stare
Don't point
Don't pick your nose
Sit up
Say please
Less noise
Shut the door behind you
Don't drag your feet
Haven't you got a hankie?
Take your hands out of your pockets
Pull up your socks
Stand up straight
Say thank you
Don't interrupt
No one thinks you're funny
Take your elbows off the table
Can't you make up your own
Mind about anything?

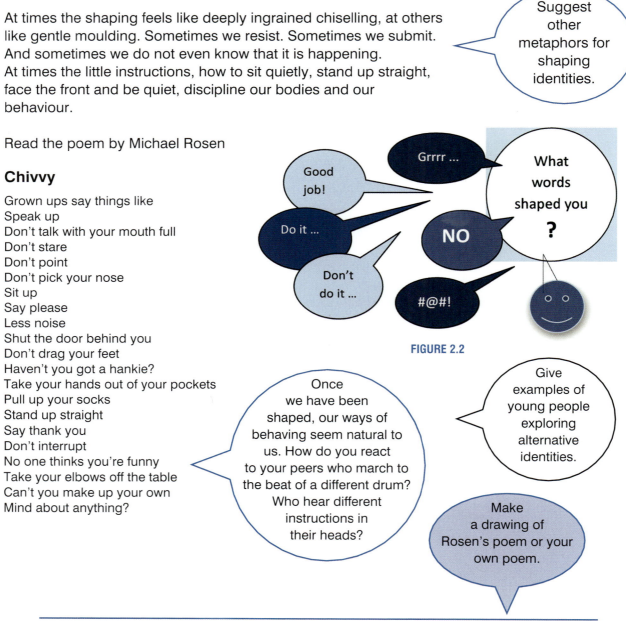

FIGURE 2.2

> Once we have been shaped, our ways of behaving seem natural to us. How do you react to your peers who march to the beat of a different drum? Who hear different instructions in their heads?

> Give examples of young people exploring alternative identities.

> Make a drawing of Rosen's poem or your own poem.

How does this poem compare with the adults in your life? Write a poem about what your parents or your teachers say to you. Begin with 'Parents say things like . . .' or 'Teachers say things like . . .'.

MANY GROUPS—MANY DIFFERENT IDENTITY POSITIONS

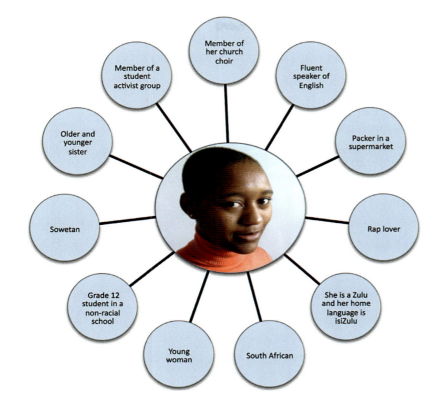

FIGURE 2.3 Thembi's identity positions

Sometimes Thembi finds that her identities clash. For example, from her school and in her student organization, she learns about equal rights for women. At home she is expected to behave like a traditional Zulu daughter and help her mother serve the men.

Now do a diagram of your identity positions. How do you use language differently in your identity positions?

1

Can you give examples of conflicting demands made by your different identity positions? Can you give other examples about other people? In which of your identity positions do you feel powerful? In which do you feel powerless?

2

You could draw identity circles of characters in novels, in soap operas, in sport. What are their identity conflicts? In which of their identities are they powerful? In which are they disempowered? How do they use language differently in different identity positions?

3

Look back at the identity portraits on page 22. Notice how each portrait emphasizes one aspect of the person's identity. Look at the collages you produced of your identities. Did you also focus on one of your identity positions or on many of them?

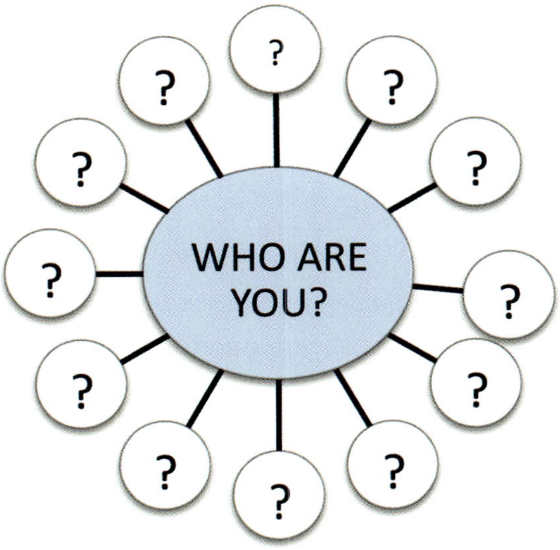

FIGURE 2.4 Your identities

IDENTITY POSITIONS IN CONFLICT

On the next page there is another poem by Michael Rosen. In this poem the boy telling the story has two different identity positions: he is both a friend and a son. He has to sort out the conflict between these two identities in order to decide what action he should take.

Relationships

1. Try to explain this kind of behaviour between friends.
2. How does Mart create tension between the narrator's two identities?
3. Do you think the narrator has a good relationship with his mother or not? Give your reasons.
4. Explain the power that each character in the poem has.
5. Compare the teasing in this poem with the teasing in *My parents kept me from children who were rough*.

Language used

6. How does Mart use language to tease? How else is language used to show the power of the different characters?
7. How well does the poet use language to show emotions and to create suspense? Find examples from the poem.
8. The poet uses a lot of direct speech. Why?

Positioning

9. The poet has used colloquial language. Where? Why?
10. What positions does the writer construct for each of the characters?
11. Writers can get power over readers by positioning them to take sides. Which character does the poet want you to side with? How do you know?
12. Does he achieve this? If so, how?

Teasing

13. Discuss the following statements.
- Teasing makes us think about social identities.
- Teasing is a way of getting power over someone.
- Silence is a way of getting power over someone.

FIGURE 2.5
The narrator in his woolly hat

DRAMA

This is a good poem to act out. You will need at least three characters: the narrator, his mother and Mart. When you dramatise a poem, you should stick as closely as you can to the words of the poem and to the situation. You have to try to capture the emotions and the mood of the poem.

ROLE PLAY

Talk about situations in your own lives in which someone was being teased or bullied. Who was being teased? About what? Why? What consequences did this have for the identities of everyone involved? How will you enact these roles? In a role play you prepare by thinking of the different roles and how people will behave in these roles, but you make up the script as you act it out.

Mart was my best friend
I thought he was great,
but one day he tried to do for me.

I had a hat—a woolly one
and I loved that hat.
It was warm and tight.
My mum knitted it
and I wore it everywhere.

One day me and Mart were out
and we were standing at the bus-stop
and suddenly
he goes and grabs my hat
and chucked it over the wall.
He thought I was going to go in there
and get it out.
He thought he'd make me do that
because he knew I liked that hat so much
I wouldn't be able to stand being without it.

He was right—
I could hardly bear it.
I was really scared I'd never get it back.
But I never let on.
I never showed it on my face.
I just waited.
'Aren't you going to get your hat?'
he says.
'Your hat's gone,' he says.
'Your hat's over the wall.'
I looked the other way.
But I could still feel on my head
how he had pulled it off.
'Your hat's over the wall,' he says.
I didn't say a thing.

Then the bus came round the corner
at the end of the road.

If I go home without my hat
I'm going to walk through the door
and mum's going to say,
'Where's your hat?'
and if I say,
'It's over the wall,'
she's going to say,
'What's it doing there?'
and I'm going to say,
'Mart chucked it over,'
and she's going to say,
'Why didn't you go for it?'
and what am I going to say then?
what am I going to say then?
The bus was coming up.

'There won't be another bus for ages,'
Mart says.

The bus was coming closer.
'You've lost your hat now,'
Mart says.

The bus stopped.
I got on
Mart got on
The bus moved off
'You've lost your hat,' Mart says.

'You've lost your hat,' Mart says.

Two stops ahead, was ours.
'Are you going indoors without it?'
Mart says
I didn't say a thing.

The bus stopped.

Mart got up
and dashed downstairs.
He'd got off one stop early.
I got off when we got to our stop.

I went home
walked through the door
'Where's your hat?' Mum says.
'Over a wall,' I said.
'What's it doing there?' she says.
'Mart chucked it over there,' I said.
'But you haven't left it there, have you?'
    she says.
'Yes,' I said.
'Well don't you ever come asking me to
    make you
anything like that again.
You make me tired you do.'

Later,
I was drinking some orange juice.
The front door-bell rang.
It was Mart. He had the hat in his hand.
He handed it me—and went.

I shut the front door—
put on the hat
and walked into the kitchen.
Mum looked up.
'You don't need to wear your hat indoors
    do you?'
she said.
'I will for a bit,' I said.
And I did.

FIGURE 2.6 'Mart was my best friend' by Michael Rosen

CONFLICTING DISCOURSES

Read the following account of *The Spear*, discuss the issues raised and then make up your own mind. Discuss the meaning created by the arrangement of the facts. Re-arrange them for a different effect.

Background information

Under Apartheid black people who were the majority of the population in South Africa were treated as inferior citizens. It was not simply that they were not allowed to vote or move freely; segregation denied them access to quality jobs, schools, hospitals and living areas reserved for whites. As if this were not bad enough, black people had to swallow scorn, humiliation and countless indignities, daily. In Europe, black bodies were exhibited in museums and circuses.

Justice Malala, writing in the *Sunday Times* newspaper, says

> Incidents, small and large, bring back that hurt, that pain, that remembrance, that once, not so long ago, we were subhuman in this country. They bring back the remembrance that the black man was viewed as a sex-obsessed, lazy . . . well animal really.
> We were not human here.
> (*Sunday Times Review*, 27 May 2012, p. 1)

The democratic elections in 1994 ended Apartheid rule and The South African Constitution became law. This Constitution includes the right to freedom of expression and the right to human dignity.

How should the courts decide when a person claims that the free expression of an artist has led to the loss of his dignity, particularly when the person making the claim is Jacob Zuma, the President of South Africa? You decide.

The Spear (2012): some of the 'facts'

- South African law recognizes polygamy as traditional law.
- President Jacob Zuma has four wives and twenty-two children.
- Zuma has thirteen children out of wedlock and several mistresses.
- The number of wives and children is a sign of wealth and status in traditional African communities.
- His critics believe that Zuma's sexual behavior is immoral.
- Before becoming President, Zuma was tried for rape and acquitted.
- In 2012, artist Brett Murray exhibited a satirical portrait, entitled *The Spear*. Copying the pose of Lenin in a famous pop-art image, Murray shows exposed genitals and a face that could be Zuma's.
- Other images in the exhibition are critical of Zuma's government and his party, the ANC.
- Many Africans, including Zuma, believe that showing a person's genitals is 'against African culture'.
- Other Africans disagree.
- The ANC took the issue to court. They wanted the picture to be taken down and for *City Press*, a newspaper marketed to African readers, to remove the image from its website.
- The painting was said to violate Zuma's right to human dignity.
- *City Press* refused to remove the image, claiming the right to freedom of expression, but eventually backed down.
- The owner of the gallery where the painting was showing supports the artist's right to freedom of expression and argues that art can and should challenge the ideas of society.
- A professor of art says this painting is a symbolic image of gendered power and not a portrait of Zuma or his actual genitals.
- Murray was accused of racism and cultural insensitivity.
- The painting went viral on the internet.
- Two men defaced the work of art, one with black paint, the other with red paint.
- The gallery agreed to take the painting down.
- The painting had been sold for R136,000 (about $18,000).
- Zuma's allies constructed Zuma as a victim of white norms and white racism.
- Some people believe that this was a strategy to re-elect Zuma.

CREATING A SENSE OF BELONGING

What is clear is that to be a member of a community you need to understand the community's 'rules', including its rules for speaking. These rules help to create *a common identity* for members of the community. How far you have to follow the rules and how far you are allowed to break the rules differs in different communities. There are also different groups within communities—and different groups have *different identities* with more or less different rules.

FIGURE 2.7 Sameness and difference

COMMON IDENTITY

In groups or pairs think about your own school, college or university. Look at its traditions and symbols. Look at the words of its songs or chants. How does your institution create an identity for itself compared with other institutions? How does your institution try to make you proud to belong to it? What teams does it have? What events and ceremonies does it arrange?

DIFFERENT IDENTITIES

Think about the students in your school, college or university. Have they divided themselves into different social groups? How? Can you identify them by the things they do? By the way they dress? By the language they use? How else can you identify them? How easy is it to get into one of these groups? What do you have to do to get into a group?

For discussion

- Why do most people need to be members of a group?
- What kinds of groups do the people you know belong to?
- Discuss the differences in the combinations of speaking/writing-doing-being-believing-valuing in the different groups that you belong to.
- Are the ways in which words, beliefs and values operate in your school or educational institution the same as, or different from, at home?

How easy or difficult is it for you to move across groups or communities that have different ways of speaking, doing, believing and valuing?

LANGUAGE—BELONGING AND EXCLUSION

Language can create a sense of belonging to a group or community. It marks who is included and at the same time who is excluded. It helps to create an 'us'—those who belong—and a 'them'—the outsiders.

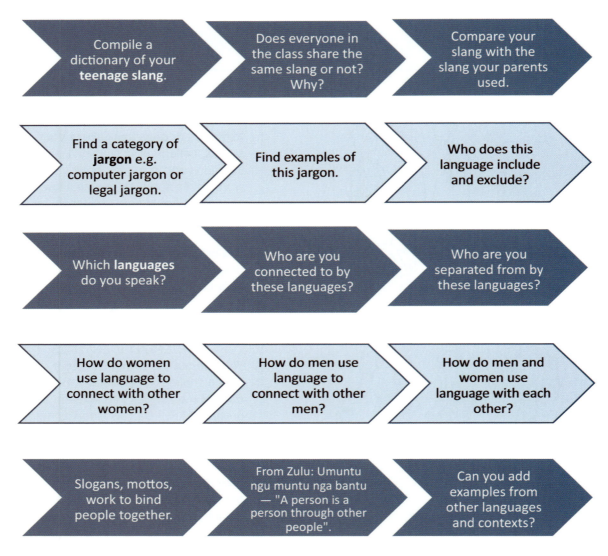

Compile a dictionary of your **teenage slang**.

Does everyone in the class share the same slang or not? Why?

Compare your slang with the slang your parents used.

Find a category of **jargon** e.g. computer jargon or legal jargon.

Find examples of this jargon.

Who does this language include and exclude?

Which **languages** do you speak?

Who are you connected to by these languages?

Who are you separated from by these languages?

How do women use language to connect with other women?

How do men use language to connect with other men?

How do men and women use language with each other?

Slogans, mottos, work to bind people together.

From Zulu: Umuntu ngu muntu nga bantu — "A person is a person through other people".

Can you add examples from other languages and contexts?

FIGURE 2.8

Can you think of other examples of language that either include or exclude? What about gang signs or the ways the characters in the Harry Potter books use language differently? What about Shakespeare's use of language in his plays or the language of disc jockeys or sports commentators? What about the languages of different school subjects? What about people in a multilingual country who do not speak or understand one another's languages?

US AND THEM

Anyone who has watched mainstream Hollywood movies understands the difference between the 'good guys' and the 'bad guys'. Who the bad guys are changes according to who is America's 'enemy' at different moments of history. The enemy is often given an offensive or derogatory name.

FIGURE 2.9 Hollywood and the dangerous Other
Source: http://nraila.org/media/2432660/terrorist.jpg.

1. Who do these names refer to? Why do you think derogatory names are often used?

2. What era is associated with each of these bad guys?

3. Describe the stereotype that goes with each of these baddies?

4. What is a stereotype?

5. Do you think that movies influence our attitudes to groups who are stereotyped?

6. Can you think of movies made in the US that challenge these representations?

7. Who are the bad guys in James Bond movies over time?

It is a pity that people tend to construct a sense of who *they* are in contrast to people who are different from them. Too often the Other is seen as a dangerous threat. Look at your own country: read your newspapers; listen to the news on TV. Who in your country is portrayed as a threat to society? Is it 'the youth'? Is it immigrants? Is it women who wear the veil? Is it a racial group? Is it foreigners? Is it criminals? Is it unemployed people? Is it people with HIV-AIDS?

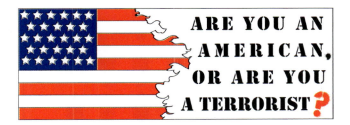

FIGURE 2.10

Make a collage using photographs, headlines, words and cartoons of the people or types of people currently constructed as the 'bad guys' in your own country or community.

WHO IS NORMAL? WE ARE NORMAL

What counts as normal is what society decides is normal. Often nature is used to justify definitions of normal.

FIGURE 2.11 Caster Semenya

Note: Caster Semenya, the South African athlete, was subjected to gender testing because her high levels of testosterone were seen to give her an unfair advantage.

FIGURE 2.12

Michael Phelps

Note: Generally, a man's arm span equals his height but Michael Phelps's arms are 6'7"—three inches more than his height. This is seen as a natural advantage.

It is clear that not all differences are equally valued. This leads to a society divided into haves and have-nots: the beautiful people who are educated and rich and powerful and those who are excluded and disadvantaged because society values them less.

Can you suggest other sets in which sub-groups do not have equal status or power?

Examine the following sets of groups and decide which group in the set has the most status and/or power in your own community? In your country? Also decide which group has the least power and/or status.

1. Men, women.
2. Managers, workers, owners.
3. Young adults, teenagers, young children.
4. Bisexuals, heterosexuals, gay men, lesbians.
5. Teachers, students.
6. Europeans, Orientals, Asians, Africans.
7. People who are able-bodied, mentally disabled, physically disabled.
8. Teachers, lawyers, doctors, accountants.
9. Urban and rural people.
10. Young men, adult women, old men.

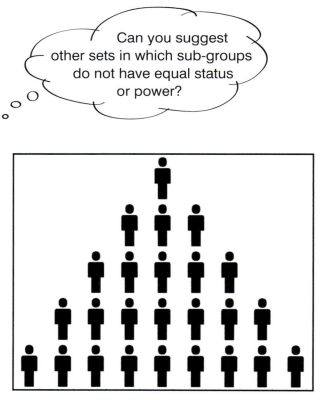

FIGURE 2.13 Human hierarchy

DIFFERENCE AS ABNORMAL

In the following article an anthropologist reports on his study of the Nacirema. Find all the descriptions that show them to be a primitive people. What does this story teach us?

Body ritual among the Nacirema by Horace Miner, 1956

Professor Linton first brought the ritual of the Nacirema to the attention of anthropologists twenty years ago (1936:326), but the culture of this people is still very poorly understood. They are a North American group living in the territory between the Canadian Cree, the Yaqui and Tarahumare of Mexico, and the Carib and Arawak of the Antilles. Little is known of their origin although tradition states that they came from the east. According to Nacirema mythology, their nation was originated by a culture hero, Notgnihsaw, who is otherwise known for two great feats of strength—the throwing of a piece of wampum across the river Pa-To-Mac and the chopping down of a cherry tree in which the Spirit of Truth resided.

Nacirema culture is characterized by a highly developed market economy. . . . While much of the people's time is devoted to economic pursuits, a large part of the fruits of these labors and a considerable portion of the day is spent on ritual activity. The focus of this activity is the human body, the appearance and health of which loom as a dominant concern in the ethos of the people. While such concern is certainly not unusual, its ceremonial aspect and associated philosophy are unique.

The fundamental belief underlying the whole system appears to be that the human body is ugly and that its natural tendency is to debility and disease. Incarcerated in such a body, man's only hope is to avert these characteristics through the use of the powerful influences of ritual and ceremony. Every household has one or more shrines in their houses, and, in fact, the opulence of a house is often referred to in terms of the number of [its] ritual centers.

The focal point of the shrine is a box or chest which is built into the wall. In this chest are kept the many charms and magical potions without which no native believes he could live. These preparations are secured from a variety of specialized practitioners.

The most powerful of these are the medicine men, whose assistance must be rewarded with substantial gifts. However, the medicine men do not provide the curative potions for their clients, but decide what the ingredients should be and then write them down in an ancient and secret language. This writing is understood only by the medicine men and by the herbalists who, for another gift, provide the required charm.

The charm is not disposed of after it has served its purpose, but is placed in the charm-box of the household shrine. We can only assume that the idea in retaining all the old magical materials is that their presence in the charm-box, before which the body rituals are conducted, will in some way protect the worshipper. . . .

Beneath the charm-box is a small font. Each day every member of the family, in succession, enters the shrine room, bows his head before the charm-box, mingles different sorts of holy water in the font, and proceeds with a brief rite of ablution.

In the hierarchy of magical practitioners, and below the medicine men in prestige, are specialists whose designation is best translated 'holy-mouth-men.' The Nacirema have an almost pathological horror of and fascination with the mouth, the condition of which is believed to have a supernatural influence on all social relationships. Were it not for the rituals of the mouth, they believe that their teeth would fall out, their gums bleed, their jaws shrink, their friends desert them, and their lovers reject them. . . .

The daily body ritual performed by everyone includes a daily mouth-rite. Despite the fact that these people are so punctilious about care of the mouth, this rite involves a practice which strikes the uninitiated stranger as revolting. It was reported to me that the ritual consists of inserting a small bundle of hog hairs into the mouth, along with certain magical powders, and then moving the bundle in a highly formalized series of gestures.[5]

FIGURE 2.14 See http://fasnafan.tripod.com/nacirema.pdf.

THE POWER OF OTHERING

RESEARCH PROJECT

History teaches us that when we see people as Other we are capable of committing terrible acts of cruelty against them. Research the ways in which people were treated as less than human in any of the following situations.

- The German concentration camps.
- The conflict between the Hutus and the Tutsis in Rwanda.
- Apartheid rule in South Africa.
- 'Ethnic cleansing' in the Serbo-Croatian conflict.

XENOPHOBIA—FEAR, DISTRUST OR HATRED OF STRANGERS

In 2008, sixty-seven people died in what came to be referred to as xenophobic attacks in South Africa. Directed at foreigners, mostly from Africa, living in some of the poorest urban areas of South Africa, hundreds of people were injured and thousands were forcibly removed from their homes. Approximately 1,400 people were arrested for crimes committed as part of the attacks—murder, attempted murder, aggravated robbery and theft.

Makwerekwere is the derogatory term used by Black South Africans to describe non-South African blacks . . . immigrants from the rest of Africa, especially Nigerians. . . . Black South Africans have found an easy explanation for the myriad problems of poverty, housing, transportation, unemployment, crime, violence, decay of public and social infrastructure. 'Ah, the *makwerekwere*!' These Nigerians are all criminals! When they are not busy trafficking drugs, they are taking over our jobs, our houses and, worse, our women. All foreigners must leave this country! (Pius Adesanmi, Nigerian writer, 19 July 2008, www.xenophobia.org.za/citizenship.htm).

Compare with Apartheid signage.

FILM STUDY

The movie *District 9* is a science fiction film set in Johannesburg that explores xenophobia. The representation of the aliens as ugly and menacing prawns serves as a verbal/visual metaphor for our terror when we have to face others who are different. The human beings who are determined to destroy this 'threat' are mean-spirited bigots who have to learn decency from the technologically advanced alien 'prawns'. WATCH THE MOVIE and discuss what it teaches us about prejudice, humanity, heroism and the relationship between us and strange others.

FIGURE 2.15 *District 9* poster

REPRESENTATIONS OF AFRICA AND AFRICANS IN THE PRESS

In 1999 Ros Adegoke looked at the ways in which foreign Africans and their countries are talked about in South African newspapers. She found that nearly 60 percent of all the reporting was negative. The following frames (discourses) occurred most often: war and violence, economic crisis, dictatorship, civil unrest and riots, corruption and crime (37 percent). Discourses such as foreign aid, political crisis, group oppression, uncivilised behaviour, poverty and underdevelopment, disaster and tragedy, and health and disease occurred with medium frequency (21 percent). Only economic irresponsibility occurred with a low frequency (0.3 percent). The only topic that consistently received neutral or positive reporting in the entire set of data was sport.

HOW TO WRITE ABOUT AFRICA

As many of these reports were based on those of international news agencies we can conclude that discourses on Africa world-wide are negative. Check your own newspapers to see if this is true.

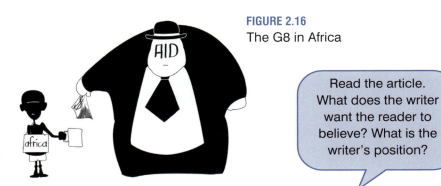

FIGURE 2.16
The G8 in Africa

Read the article. What does the writer want the reader to believe? What is the writer's position?

How to write about Africa, Binyavanga Wainainina, Kenya, 1992

Always use the word Africa or Darkness or Safari in your title. Subtitles may include the words 'Zanzibar', 'Masai', 'Zulu', 'Zambesi', 'Congo', 'Nile', 'Big', 'Sky', 'Shadow', 'Drum', 'Sun' or 'Bygone'. Also useful are words such as 'Guerillas', 'Timeless', 'Primordial', and 'Tribal'. Note that 'People' means Africans who are not black, while 'The People' means black Africans.

Never have a picture of a well-adjusted African on the cover of your book, unless that African won the Nobel Prize. An AK-47, prominent ribs, naked breasts: use these. If you must include an African make sure you get one in Masai, Zulu or Dogon dress.

In your text treat Africa as if it were one country. It is hot and dusty with huge herds of animals and tall, thin people who are starving. Or it is hot and steamy with very short people who eat primates. Don't get bogged down with precise descriptions. Africa is big: 54 countries, 900 million people who are too busy starving and dying and warring and emigrating to read your book. The continent is full of deserts, jungles, highlands, savannahs and many other things but your reader does not care about that, so keep your descriptions romantic and evocative and unparticular.

Make sure you show how Africans have music and rhythm deep in their souls and eat things no other humans eat. Do not mention rice and beef and wheat; monkey brain is the African cuisine of choice, along with goat, snake, worms and grubs and all manner of game meat. Make sure you show how you are able to eat such food without flinching, and describe how you learn to enjoy it—because you care. . . .

Among your characters you must always include The Starving African, who wanders the refugee camps, and waits for the benevolence of the West. Her children have flies on their eyelids and pot bellies, and her breasts are flat and empty. She must look utterly helpless. She can have no past, no history; such diversions ruin the dramatic moment. Moans are good.

See www.granta.com/Archive/92/How-to-Write-about-Africa/Page-1.

TOPDOGS HAVE POWER OVER UNDERDOGS

In order to discuss power differences between groups in society, it is useful to have some terminology. I will call groups that have power *dominant groups* or *topdogs*, and groups who have less power than the dominant groups *subordinate groups* or *underdogs*. The expressions 'topdogs' and 'underdogs' come from the sport of dog fighting. The losing dog is called the underdog and the winner is called the topdog. These expressions may be used for people. I will use 'topdog' to refer to a person who belongs to a dominant group and I will use 'underdog' to refer to a person who belongs to a dominated or oppressed group. People are usually not topdogs or underdogs in all their different identities. For example, a Basotho may be oppressed at work on the grounds of his race, his language and his skills. In his community he may be dominant because of his gender, his literacy and his age.

In pairs think about your own lives

1. Given that we all have many different identities, in which of your identities do you feel like a topdog?
2. In which identities do you feel like an underdog?
3. Who is the topdog in your family in most situations?
4. Name a situation in which someone else is topdog.
5. Amongst your friends is there competition to be topdog?
6. In your school how do students become topdogs?
7. In your school how do teachers become topdogs?
8. How do the topdogs you know treat the underdogs?
9. How do the topdogs you know talk to the underdogs?
10. Do you sometimes feel like a middle dog—neither a topdog nor an underdog?

FIGURE 2.17 Topdogs and underdogs

Feminists believe that the following set of opposites is regularly used to represent women as the 'weaker sex'.

ACTIVE	PASSIVE
knowledge	ignorance
higher up	lower down
positive, good	negative, bad
mind	body
rational	irrational
order	chaos
objective	subjective
fact	fiction
goals	processes
light	dark
writing	speaking
public domain	domestic domain
detached	attached
permanence	change
hard	soft
independent	dependent
individual	social

Which are the male and female sides of this table? How do you know? What are the effects of representing gender in this way?

Apply the different sides of this table to other dominant and dominated groups: rich/poor; colonizers/colonized; urban/rural; white/black; educated/uneducated; hetero and homosexual.

FIGURE 2.18 Binary thinking

FIGURE 2.19 Gay rights march by Matt Sandham

DEFENDING THE UNDERDOG

Read 'The Music Lesson'. While reading, imagine that you are a student in this class. What action could you take to support Mark, the underdog, who is being bullied and humiliated by his teacher? In groups, dramatise this scene but change it so that instead of the students being bystanders, one or more of them intervenes to help Mark. The intervention should be one that we can believe.

The Music Lesson by Sarah Stucki

I don't remember the words that were spoken, or if there were any, but I'll always remember his face. His tears. His sobs.

The choir room was extraordinarily noisy. The excitement of a new day was rushing through everyone. There was so much energy in the air. Enough to make lights shine and fires to start miraculously on their own. It was the perfect day for a complete disaster.

Mr Dunn, the bald, squatty man, lined us up how we sang. The good ones were in the middle, bad ones on the sides, and, of course, his star, his daughter, Brittany, right in front even though she was tall and made it difficult for anyone to be seen behind her.

'All right, class, quiet down.' He spoke in his fake, confident voice, the voice that made people squirm and their blood boil.

'Let's begin with scales. Ready and . . .' He tapped his baton on the music stand. He gripped it as though it held all the power in the world, his power that decided our self-esteem.

'La la la la la la la la la.' We were running through the non-thought-containing notes. Clearing our throats to reach the high ones. Quietly bowing our heads for the low ones. Laughing when we made a mistake because we knew we were horrible. So did Mr Dunn.

'Ha ha ha ha.' Loud laughter burst from someone to the left of me. I turned to look and see who it was. My face turned red. It was Mark. My crush on him was given away by my bright face. Suddenly, a loud tapping. I whirled around to look at Mr Dunn pounding on the music stand for us to stop with our scales.

'Who was laughing just now?' His veins stuck out of his stubby neck. Silence. 'Who was it?' He struck the stand with his baton. His eyes searched the risers for the guilty party. The person for whom the lecture would be worthy.

I felt his eyes pass over me. I was afraid for Mark because I just knew that Mr Dunn would figure out it was him. I guess it didn't help much that 59 out of the 60 choir students were staring straight at Mark.

'Mark Hubble.' His voice boomed throughout the auditorium. 'What was so funny, Mr Hubble? Why don't you share it with the class?' He stared at Mark with a smirk on his face. Mark just stared at his feet. 'Excuse me, Mark, are you deaf? What was so funny?'

A mumble came from Mark's serious face. 'Nothing,' he said.

'Nothing, huh? Well, if it was just nothing, then why don't you come and show us how well you can sing?' He made this statement as though he were a god. 'Come on, Mark. Stand here and sing your scales for the class.' He pointed to a place in front of the music stand.

Mark was a good guy. He obeyed his teachers. He was never mean at all. He was 'fortunate' to be at our school because he was from a reservation in Arizona. So, of course, he went to the music stand and stood before his peers. Us.

'You may begin now,' Mr Dunn spoke bluntly. The piano player began the run through the notes as Mark whispered the scale. 'Sing louder, Mark, we can't hear you.' Mark sang a little louder. Tears began to fall from his eyes. 'Mark, you can sing louder. We heard you loudly before when you were laughing.' Mark was crying harder now. Sobs began escaping from him.

He was very embarrassed, and I didn't blame him for crying. I would have too if Mr Dunn had treated me like Mark, and I feel today that the only reason he was so mean to Mark was because Mark was Native-American.

Mark never finished those scales that day, and he never came back again. I don't blame him for that either.

Sarah Stucki was a junior at Jefferson High School in Portland, Oregon, when she wrote this piece as part of an 'Acting for Justice' unit. See Christensen L. (2000) *Reading, Writing and Rising Up*. Milwaukee: Rethinking Schools.

Write your own story about being bullied or excluded or about witnessing someone else being singled out for unfair treatment. Compare Mark with the narrator in 'Mart was my Best Friend' on p. 39.

CHANGING IDENTITIES

What can we do if we find ourselves part of an oppressed group? What are our options?

RESEARCH PROJECT

What choices have been made by liberation movements and their leaders in the past? Do research on social transformation in South Africa or the Civil Rights Movement in the US or the role played by Ghandi in India. Social transformation on this scale is what we call big *P* politics.

OPTION 1: LEAVE THE GROUP

1985 had at least 1 000 'Chameleons'

Political staff

PARLIAMENT – More than 1 000 people officially changed colour last year. They were reclassified from one race group to another by the stroke of a government pen … [in] what is dubbed the chameleon dance.

The Minister of Home Affairs, Mr Stoffel Botha disclosed that in 1985

- 702 coloured people turned white.
- 19 whites became coloured.
- One Indian became white.
- Three Chinese became white.
- 50 Indians became Malay.
- 43 coloureds became Indians.
- 30 Malays went Indian.
- 249 blacks became coloureds.
- 20 coloureds became black.
- Two blacks became 'other' Asians.
- One black was classified Griqua.
- 11 coloureds became Chinese.
- Three coloureds went Malay.
- One Chinese became coloured.
- Eight Malays became coloured.
- Three blacks were classed as Malay.
- No blacks became white and no whites became black.

FIGURE 2.20 The *Star*, 21 March 1986

In South Africa under Apartheid rule, a law known as the Population Registration Act required people to be classified according to race at birth. In addition, the Group Areas Act governed where people of different races had to live. People who were not classified white were given separate townships to live in outside of the cities. Some jobs were reserved for white people only, as were parks, public transport, schools and hospitals. People of different race groups were not allowed to have sex or get married according to the Mixed Marriages Act.

FIGURE 2.21 The chameleon dance

1. How do you think the government decided who could be reclassified? What does this tell us about racial categorization? How scientific is it?
2. Why do you think no blacks became white and no whites became black?
3. How do you think families felt about relatives who opted to be reclassified?
4. Why might people have made this choice?

RENAMING OUR IDENTITIES

OPTION 2: CONSTRUCT THE GROUP POSITIVELY

The gay-pride movement and the black consciousness movement chose this option.

I am what I am
I am my own special creation
So come take a look
Give me the hook
Or the ovation
It's my world that I want to have a little pride in
My world and it's not a place I have to hide in
Life's not worth a damn
Till you can say
I am what I am

I am what I am
I don't want praise, I don't want pity
I bang my own drum
Some thinks it's noise
I think it's pretty
And so what if I love each sparkle and each bangle
Why not try to see things from a different angle
Your life is a sham till you can shout out
I am what I am

I am what I am
And what I am
Needs no excuses
I deal my own deck
Sometimes the ace
Sometimes the deuces
It's one life and there's no return and no deposit
One life so it's time to open up your closet
Life's not worth a damn till you can shout out
I am what I am

I am what I am
And what I am needs no excuses
I deal my own deck
Sometimes the ace
Sometimes the deuces
It's one life and there's no return and no deposit
One life so it's time to open up your closet
Life's not worth a damn, till you can shout out
I am what I am.

See http://lyrics.doheth.co.uk./

Biko: I think that the slogan 'black is beautiful' is serving a very important aspect of our attempt to get at our humanity. You are challenging the very root of the back man's belief about himself. When you say 'black is beautiful' what in fact you are saying to him is: man, you are okay as you are, begin to look upon yourself as a human being. In a sense the term 'black is beautiful' challenges exactly that belief which makes someone negate himself. ...

Judge: Now why do you refer to you people as 'black'?

Biko: Historically, we have been defined as black people, and when we reject the term non-white and we take ourselves the right to call ourselves what we think we are, we choose this one precisely because we feel it is most accommodating.

Source: Steve Biko. SASO/BPC Trial, May 1976.

Why do you think gay pride adopted this song as its rallying cry?

Black is beautiful is a cultural movement begun in the US in the 1960s by African Americans. It reclaims black as a positive marker of identity and it rejects the belief that black people's natural features such as skin colour, facial features and hair are inherently ugly.

1. What can be gained from constructing a positive self-representation for one's group?

2. What are the limitations of this approach?

3. How have other oppressed groups used this approach to reconstruct their group's image?

4. Should perpetrators of serious crimes (murderers, rapists, thieves) be allowed to rename themselves once rehabilitated?

CHANGING THE POWER RELATIONS THAT AFFECT IDENTITY

OPTION 3: WORK TOWARDS EQUAL RIGHTS FOR USING LANGUAGE

Topdogs often use their power to name others. When underdogs decide to name themselves or the groups they belong to, this is a powerful form of resistance and of identifying one's self positively. Here are some examples of groups renaming themselves. Can you think of others?

Chicano ➔ Hispanic ➔ Latino	ladies ➔ women	Indians ➔ Native Americans
non-whites ➔ Bantu ➔ African	handicapped ➔ disabled	queers ➔ gays and lesbians

Naming is only part of the ways in which language is used to maintain the power of topdogs. Answer the following questions. Base your answers on careful observation of people you know.

1. Who gives orders or instructions?
2. Who speaks? Who speaks the most?
3. Who interrupts?
4. Who speaks hesitantly?
5. Who speaks in their home language?
6. Who chooses the topics to talk about?
7. Who calls who by their first names? Who does not?
8. Whose voices are listened to and believed?
9. Who decides who speaks?

1. Do people have these rights as individuals or as members of social groups?
2. Can you think of other inequalities in language rights?
3. How do your own different identity positions affect your language rights?

OPTION 4: CHANGING THE POWER OF THE GROUP

People have found ways of challenging the power that others have over them, often by working together. Here are some examples: the women's movement, which fought for the vote and equal pay for equal work; workers' unions, which negotiate fair pay and reasonable working conditions; consumer boycotts against high food prices; the gay and lesbian movement's struggle for civil rights; and the liberation movements that you have already researched. Where groups are struggling for equality, rather than dominance, they contribute to the development of a world that is fair and just. Often people who are interested in social justice support their causes, even though they may not themselves be members of the group.

Vivian Vasquez worked with a class of 3–5-year-old students in Canada. The students were upset when 4-year-old Anthony told them during a class meeting that he had not eaten anything at the school barbecue because he was a vegetarian. In discussion with Vivian the children decided on ways in which they could make sure that their school (and neighbouring schools) provided food for vegetarians. They did research on vegetarians in the library and found out why people choose to be vegetarian; they conducted a survey to see how many people in their school were vegetarians; they wrote letters; they wrote a petition. They brought about change in their school.

Could you do something similar?

Section 3: Language and language varieties

Section 3 focuses on the status of different languages and tackles the question of language hierarchies. It problematizes the notion of a 'standard' variety in order to unpack issues of status, access and power. It begins with an activity that immediately makes the link between our repertoire of languages and our identities.

Choosing signs

In the introduction and in the previous sections, I made the case that text-makers select signs from a range of possible options and that these 'choices' affect how the text is positioned and positioning. Here the focus is on how the 'choice' of which language or language variety to use affects meaning. I have put the word *choice* in quotes to remind us that often the discourses we inhabit influence our choices below the level of consciousness.

Languages choose us

This is particularly true of the languages we speak. We do not choose the languages into which we are born. Some of us acquire many languages naturally because we live in multilingual communities. Migrants usually have to acquire additional languages, sometimes in order to survive. Others have to make a deliberate effort to learn additional languages. It is important to recognize that we do not all have equal access to the languages we need or would like to learn.

Similarly, we acquire the variety of the language that we hear around us. For example, I grew up speaking Standard South African English, the children I taught in London spoke Cockney and many African Americans use Ebonics.

Language and identity

The languages we speak are therefore bound up with our sense of self—they connect us to our families, our schooling, our neighbourhoods, our life histories. They connect us to time and our movements through space and they are deeply embodied. They encode values and world views together with norms for interacting with others in different places.

Deciding what language to use

Choosing which language or which variety to use in particular situations involves what is often a split-second decision based on an analysis of all the social factors that affect communication. When we produce spoken texts this decision is ongoing: Should I code-switch? Should I use the standard variety or my own dialect? How formal must I be? Whose language must I use? In written texts I have to imagine my audience and decide whether to choose a global language, a national language or a local variety or a mixture.

Are all languages equal?

From the point of view of linguists no language is better than another, no accent is more harmonious, no variety is ungrammatical. No language is more logical or more beautiful. However, even if languages are linguistically equal, they are not equally valued in society.

The status of a language is affected by both its economic power and our attitudes to it. If we believe that a particular language is a sign of education or sophistication then we give it status simply by valuing it above other languages. Section 3 looks carefully at social attitudes to different languages and different varieties. It examines social hierarchies of language, linguistic prejudice and linguistic dominance, and it explores the issues of correctness and appropriateness.

The sequence of ideas in this section

Section 3 starts with your linguistic repertoire—the languages you speak. It considers its relative power and the impact it has if one's home language is or is not a powerful language. You are also asked to work out criteria for deciding on the power of different languages (pp. 55–59). Page 56 looks at how our attitudes give a language power.

Standard English is the variety that is often thought of as 'correct' or 'proper' English. It is powerful because it is the variety spoken by elites and provides access to elite jobs. By extension, non-standard varieties are considered by some, such as Bill Cosby for example, to be wrong, rather than just different (p. 59 and p. 63).

Our attitudes, including our attitudes to language, are often based on prejudice (p. 57) and they can be used for linguistic profiling (p. 59)—deciding that someone is up to no good because of the way in which they speak.

Because dialects (p. 60) are often the variety spoken at home, we are attached to them. They are a part of who we are and give us a sense of identity and of belonging (p. 62). Yet these are often the varieties that are deemed inappropriate in school and for access to high-status employment.

Who decides what is appropriate, where and when, are the people who are powerful in the places where those varieties are used. So teachers may be powerful in the classroom where they make students speak 'properly'; but that is not necessarily the

dialect you need to survive on the playground (pp. 63–64).

Because different varieties and different languages are needed for different contexts it is important to be multilingual and to have a number of languages and varieties in your repertoire (p. 67). That way you can increase your chances of fitting in easily in more situations. However, multilingualism *per se* does not guarantee greater access or power.

Page 65 suggests that variety is also what keeps language interesting and culture alive. Joe Khumalo argues that in switching to English the new black elite in South Africa is losing touch with their roots.

Pages 68–69 focus on the dominance of English in the world. As English becomes a global language it continues to split into a range of varieties now known as World Englishes (p. 70). This complicates matters further: what counts as standard is different in different places and what is accepted as standard in Nigeria or India may be viewed as sub-standard in Britain. The norms of the periphery are not always the norms of the centre.

Power, diversity, access, design/redesign

This section works mostly with language and identity. It shows how linguistic diversity can lead to differences in power and access. Not all languages or all dialects are valued equally. This can lead to us profiling people we meet and dismissing or overvaluing them based on the way they speak. As a result the language or variety we choose to use is one of the ways in which we design our identities and other people's judgements about who we are. It is a powerful force in constructing who is *us* and who is *them*.

THE LANGUAGES WE SPEAK

Language biography

Write the story of how you came to speak the languages you speak. *These questions will help you to begin.* What language did you learn to speak first? Why that language? Can you read and write that language? Perhaps you learnt two first languages simultaneously. How did that happen? Then discuss all the other languages that you understand, speak, read or write and account for this in relation to your own history of community, and movement from place to place. What language do you think in? Do you dream in a language? Does language contribute to defining your identity? In what way/s? Do you feel powerful in all your languages? Under what circumstances?

FIGURE 3.1 Identity crisis
Source: www.weheartit.com.

The power of different languages

1. List all the languages spoken by members of your class. Count how many languages there are.
2. In groups, rank these languages from the most powerful at the top to the least powerful at the bottom. Equally powerful languages can be banded together.
3. What criteria did you use to assess the power of a language?
4. Does a language have the same power in a different place?
5. Compare your criteria and your rankings with another group and then with the class.
6. How does it affect you if you speak a powerful language? How does it affect you if you do not?

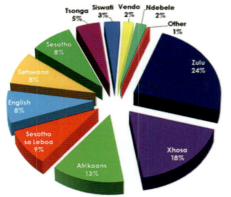

FIGURE 3.2 Languages spoken in South Africa

Research project

Find out which ten languages in the world have the most speakers.

There are more people who speak English as an additional language than there are native speakers of the language. Find out how this has affected English.

Find out which languages are endangered and why.

Find the language statistics for your country.

ATTITUDES TOWARDS LANGUAGES

Read the following statements. Decide which ones you agree or disagree with and write a short list of the reasons why you feel this way. Debate some of these with people who have a different opinion from your own. After the debate think about what may have made people change their minds.

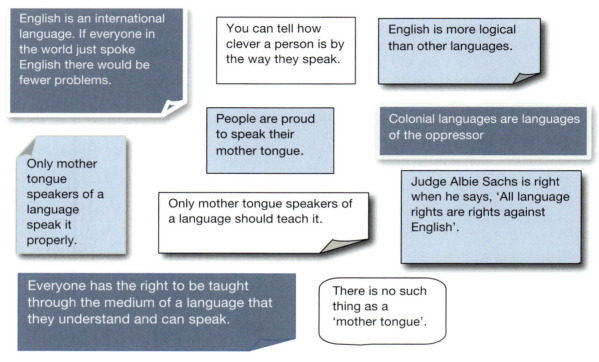

FIGURE 3.3 Language attitudes

These statements reveal a lot about our attitudes towards languages and to their speakers. We can have positive and negative attitudes towards languages, speakers of other languages, how people speak a language, and how well we think they know it. Sometimes our attitudes are informed by a limited knowledge of language and people. Think carefully about what you based your opinions on. Did you have real evidence to substantiate your points? How much has your own language history affected these opinions?

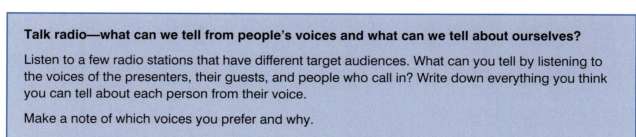

Talk radio—what can we tell from people's voices and what can we tell about ourselves?

Listen to a few radio stations that have different target audiences. What can you tell by listening to the voices of the presenters, their guests, and people who call in? Write down everything you think you can tell about each person from their voice.

Make a note of which voices you prefer and why.

Look at your list again. Which points are facts that you know are true (i.e. the speaker is an adult) and how many are value judgements (they have a nice voice, they sound clever)?

LINGUISTIC PREJUDICE

Language is a reflection of a people. For example, French culture is perceived as high quality, its cuisine is considered to be great, its fashion's avant garde, so if a person speaks with a French accent, it's perceived to be very positive because the people are perceived positively.

But if a group is considered to be ignorant, primitive, backward, ill-informed, then their language is given similar attributes. The problem is that African American people and Black people around the world are perceived by dominant societies to be inferior, so their language is perceived in a similar way.

(Dr Orlando Taylor)

All of us have perceptions about speakers of other languages. These negative perceptions are often based on stereotypes. When we judge people as stupid, slow or uneducated when they talk, we show our linguistic prejudices.

All of us have some linguistic prejudice. Although we know that we should not make racist or sexist remarks, we often say terrible things about the way people speak. Who are you linguistically prejudiced against? How can you challenge your linguistic prejudice?

Linguistic prejudice often comes from dominant groups who believe their practices are correct. This thinking also affects how marginal groups see themselves. How is Cosby, who is an African American, linguistically prejudiced? What could you tell Cosby to challenge his beliefs about African American English? Can you find similar examples where you live?

We've got to take the neighborhood back. We've got to go in there. Just forget telling your child to go to the Peace Corps. It's right around the corner. It's standing on the corner. It can't speak English. It doesn't want to speak English. I can't even talk the way these people talk: 'Why you ain't where you is go ra?' I don't know who these people are. And I blamed the kid until I heard the mother talk. Then I heard the father talk. This is all in the house. You used to talk a certain way on the corner and you got into the house and switched to English. Everybody knows it's important to speak English except these knuckleheads. You can't land a plane with, 'Why you ain't . . .'. You can't be a doctor with that kind of [rubbish] coming out of your mouth.

(Extract from speech given by Bill Cosby, 17 May 2004)[6]

LANGUAGE VARIETIES: DIALECTS

People and groups of people often speak the same language in different ways. These differences can be identified by their *accents*, the way they *pronounce* certain words, variations in *grammar* and the *vocabulary* they use. When a group uses the same variations in the way they speak, we call the variety a *dialect*. Everyone speaks a dialect and everyone has an accent. Dialects are influenced by geography, gender, class, race, age and ethnicity. These language varieties are not all equally valued in society.

The variety that becomes the standard form is taught in schools and used in writing. Just as people have attitudes that some languages are better than others, many people think the standard variety is better than non-standard varieties. However, with a world language such as English, the standard English variety accepted in one place may be looked down upon in another.

When linguists study dialects they can show that they all have rules and are used systematically. Although non-standard dialects may be different from the standard form, they have their own internal logic. Because we are taught the rules and patterns of the standard form at school we assume that other ways of speaking do not have rules and are incorrect. Which varieties are prestigious and which are not in your country?

African American English is a dialect that has been studied by linguists. Look at the extract taken from comedian Chris Rock. What features of his language would you say are systematically used by speakers of this dialect? (Think about his use of vocabulary, pronunciation and grammar.) How does his use of African American English challenge dominant cultural and language norms?

Yeah, I love being famous. It's almost like being white, y'know? People are nice to ya, they give you the benefit o' the doubt. . . . You drive a flash car down the freeway and the cops'll pull y'over and before they even look they like 'What are you doing?' and then they see it's you and they like 'Awww man, it's Chris Rock, it's okay, man we thought you was a nigga'.

(Chris Rock, http://thinkexist.com/quotation)

FIGURE 3.4 Chris Rock

Analyse the picture

1. Who is being arrested? What can you tell about this man? (Age, race, gender, class).
2. Who is arresting him? What can you tell about them?
3. Where is he being arrested?
4. Is it possible that, unlike Chris Rock, he is not black and famous, he is just black?
5. What is meant by racial profiling?[7]

FIGURE 3.5 Henry Louis Gates   *Source*: www.time.com.

LINGUISTIC PROFILING

Read the article below.

'Testers Posing as Katrina Survivors Encounter "Linguistic Profiling"', Lorinda M. Bullock, 20 August 2006

As the one-year anniversary of Hurricane Katrina approaches, displaced Americans from Louisiana and the Gulf Coast have been slowly rebuilding their lives and looking for a place to call home.

While Katrina's Black victims shop the housing market, calling realtors and potential landlords, one thing may be standing between them and their new homes even before an appointment is made or paperwork filled out—their voice.

It's called linguistic profiling.

A study of five states done by the National Fair Housing Alliance and linguistics expert John Baugh revealed in 66 percent of phone tests administered by White and Black testers inquiring about housing as Katrina survivors, 'White callers were favored over African-American callers,' the report said.

Shanna Smith, president of NFHA, said 'It's a different kind of behavior in discrimination from the 70s until now where they would just simply say we don't have anything available. Now they try not to trigger suspicion so they may say when do you need it or I won't know until the end of the month, when in fact, they may have three or four apartments available right now.'

Smith said another tactic that is used is asking a potential renter or buyer for their name to be put on a waiting list, 'Names that didn't sound middle America White didn't get the return emails about availability.'

Baugh found the questions from landlords varied, depending on the voice they heard. Baugh, who flawlessly uses three different voices— a 'Latino rendition, modified African-American rendition and standard English'—always kept the opening line the same, 'Hello, I'm calling about the apartment you have advertised in the paper.'

While Baugh says Black and Hispanic people in the U.S. are discriminated against heavily because of their voice, he makes it very clear that linguistic profiling is not even limited to just those groups. Smith, who is White, said 'I've been doing testing where people say, you're going to like it here. We don't rent to Blacks. White people hear this all the time.' She estimates there are close to 4 million instances of discrimination that occur annually in the U.S.

While everyone 'accommodates linguistically' depending on the situation, be it a job interview or joking with friends, Baugh said people should not have to hide who they are but shouldn't be naive to society's biases either. 'People should not feel they need to mask their linguistic background. You should be free to speak in whatever way is comfortable for you and your fellow citizens don't misjudge you.'

1. What is linguistic profiling?

2. In this article people who are looking for housing are linguistically profiled and discriminated against. Why are white callers favoured over other racial groups? Which groups are likely to be negatively profiled in your community or your country?

3. What other examples can you think of where a person may be linguistically profiled when they make a phone call?

4. Have you ever been linguistically profiled on the phone? What happened? Have you ever done this to someone else? What do these incidents reveal about our linguistic prejudice?

NON-STANDARD VARIETIES AS A MARKER OF SOLIDARITY

Read the following extract from Sting's autobiography *Broken Music*. Sting grew up in a working-class suburb in Newcastle in England. Before he was a famous musician he acted to make extra money. In the extract he is at an acting audition talking to the director, Frank Roddam.

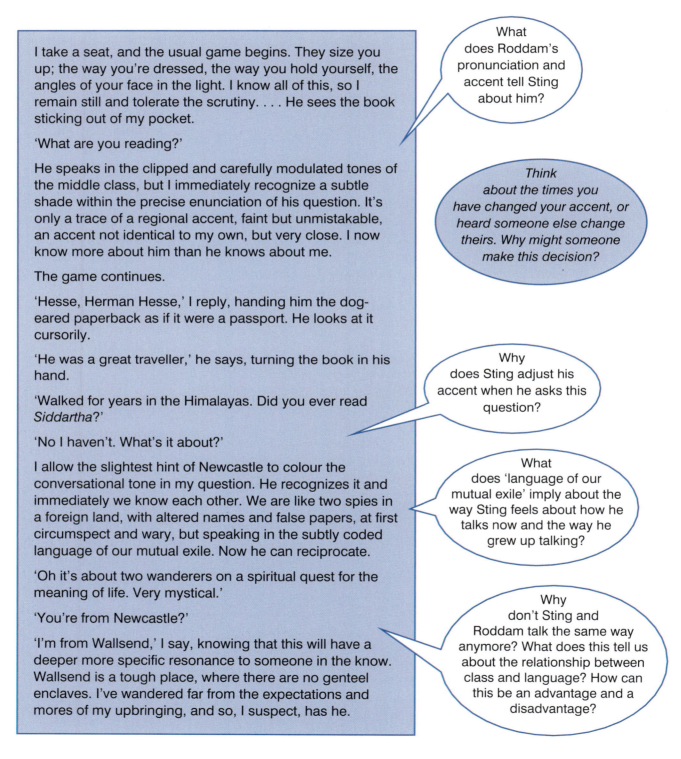

I take a seat, and the usual game begins. They size you up; the way you're dressed, the way you hold yourself, the angles of your face in the light. I know all of this, so I remain still and tolerate the scrutiny. . . . He sees the book sticking out of my pocket.

'What are you reading?'

> What does Roddam's pronunciation and accent tell Sting about him?

He speaks in the clipped and carefully modulated tones of the middle class, but I immediately recognize a subtle shade within the precise enunciation of his question. It's only a trace of a regional accent, faint but unmistakable, an accent not identical to my own, but very close. I now know more about him than he knows about me.

The game continues.

> *Think about the times you have changed your accent, or heard someone else change theirs. Why might someone make this decision?*

'Hesse, Herman Hesse,' I reply, handing him the dog-eared paperback as if it were a passport. He looks at it cursorily.

'He was a great traveller,' he says, turning the book in his hand.

'Walked for years in the Himalayas. Did you ever read *Siddartha*?'

'No I haven't. What's it about?'

> Why does Sting adjust his accent when he asks this question?

I allow the slightest hint of Newcastle to colour the conversational tone in my question. He recognizes it and immediately we know each other. We are like two spies in a foreign land, with altered names and false papers, at first circumspect and wary, but speaking in the subtly coded language of our mutual exile. Now he can reciprocate.

> What does 'language of our mutual exile' imply about the way Sting feels about how he talks now and the way he grew up talking?

'Oh it's about two wanderers on a spiritual quest for the meaning of life. Very mystical.'

'You're from Newcastle?'

'I'm from Wallsend,' I say, knowing that this will have a deeper more specific resonance to someone in the know. Wallsend is a tough place, where there are no genteel enclaves. I've wandered far from the expectations and mores of my upbringing, and so, I suspect, has he.

> Why don't Sting and Roddam talk the same way anymore? What does this tell us about the relationship between class and language? How can this be an advantage and a disadvantage?

APPROPRIATENESS AND COMMUNICATIVE COMPETENCE

Our language behaviour is shaped in the same way as our other behaviour is shaped. According to a linguist called Dell Hymes, part of learning a language is learning when to speak as well as how to use the language when we do speak. He called this 'communicative competence'. Dell Hymes said:

> Children acquire competence as to when to speak, when not, and as to what to talk about with whom, when, where and in what manner.

We learn these rules of use by growing up in a society that teaches us how to use language appropriately according to its rules. These rules are not written down but our family, our friends and our teachers make it clear to us how they expect us to behave. In addition to learning how to make grammatical sentences, children also learn how to make appropriate sentences. Unfortunately what counts as appropriate does not always travel well.

You used to talk a certain way on the corner and you got into the house and switched to English. Everybody knows it's important to speak English except these knuckleheads. You can't land a plane with, 'Why you ain't . . .'. You can't be a doctor with that kind of [rubbish] coming out of your mouth.

(Extract from speech given by Bill Cosby, 17 May 2004)

Madam and Eve is a comic strip that satirises life in South Africa. Eve is Madam's domestic worker. Here Madam comes to Eve's 'lemonade stand' to buy language lessons.

1. Where does the humour lie in the cartoon?
2. Do the writers of Madam and Eve agree with Cosby or not?
3. What do you think?

FIGURE 3.6 *Madam and Eve*

Learning the rules

1. Write down a list of the rules for speaking in your family and community. Choose a particular event or activity (e.g. meal times) and then think about when are you allowed to speak, when are you not allowed to speak, what can you talk about, who can you talk to, and how you are expected to talk. How did you learn these rules?

2. Then share your answers with a classmate. Which rules are similar and which are different? How do families teach their children rules for speaking and behaving that leads to communicative competence in the communities to which they belong?

3. Can you think of any instances where the rules you learnt for your language were the wrong ones in a different context?

4. Can you think of any instances where the rules you learnt for your language were wrong when applied to a different language? What happened?

APPROPRIATENESS AND POWER

What is correct English?

If we think about the meaning of communicative competence then the answer to the question would be 'It depends on the context': where you are and what the expectations for speaking are. But when we learn to write in a language at school we are taught the standard form. This variety is usually associated with the educated middle class and is socially prestigious. It has a standard set of rules for grammar, vocabulary, spelling and punctuation, but not accent. There is not one correct version of English though. There are different Standard Englishes, e.g. British, American, South African, Australian. Americans will be *in* their *favorite* shop, the British will be *at* their *favourite* shop. South Africans have *cell phones*, Australians have *mobile* phones. South Africans wear *takkies*, Americans wear *sneakers* and the British wear *trainers*.

1.

Who gets to decide which variety gets to be the standard form? Who gets to decide what is appropriate? How does power affect whose norms of use become the socially accepted norms?

2.

Give examples of whose ways of using language wins out when people come from communities with different rules?

3.

How do people break the rules? Why do people break the rules? What happens when people break the rules? Can breaking the rules lead to changing the rules?

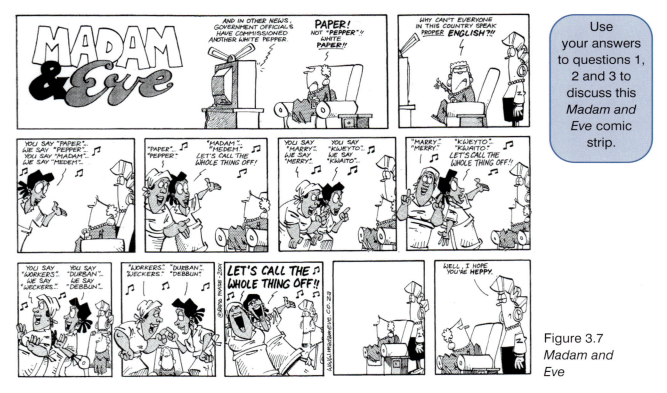

Use your answers to questions 1, 2 and 3 to discuss this *Madam and Eve* comic strip.

Figure 3.7
Madam and Eve

How much time, if any, is given to working with non-standard varieties of English in your English classroom?

If you do work with non-standard varieties what kind of exercises are you doing? What does this tell you?

JOE'S BEAT

In a room full of shabbily dressed uncles, aunts and oumas, the SUBURBAN youngsters swagger snootily among the RIFFRAFF. Their fatcat parents, SHAMED and AGGRIEVED, berate their brood for not greeting their elderly relatives …
TYINI, UNZIMA LOMTHWALO!

Joe's Beat

Suburbia? Forget it, mpintshi yam, that's for the new gravy cats. I tell you, broer, life is a real gas in the ghetto. Chicken gizzards, mala mogodu, atchaar, skaapkop and machangaan wors washed down with chibuku and mageu to the backdrop of scamtho and kwaito music. I tell you, mtshana, life is great in the hood. What more could 'n arme darkie want?

Come Friday and it's fill up the table and count the empties because it's pay day and the "weekend tycoons" have money like dust. Ziyamporoma! The airwaves offer eardrum-shattering kwaito and rap sounds as each ghetto household competes with the next for volume supremacy.

On the streets AKs are blazing and the flash guys, the snazzily dressed amagents, are cruising dangerously in their BMs, much to the envy of the girls and All Star sneaker-clad jitas.

Out in the 'burbs the new fatcats who were weaned on chicken legs and pap are battling to shake down the effects of squawking in tsotsi taal and scamtho, while waging an uphill struggle to get the hang of Mozart and the arts. Big deal! But for 'n fly ghetto laaitie this quiet life is humdrum, mtshana.

Bored with champagne, caviar and ukukhumtsha, they sneak into the dark ghetto in their Pajeros and Audi A4s for their rare dose of soul food, pap and morogo, stokvels, tebellos, amadlozi ceremonies and ever-plentiful mgosi. But there's the rub.

With their kids who have imbibed the suburban culture, going back to the ghetto is a horrific culture shock to the "nose brigade" who express themselves in vogue Oxford accents.

First they will have to contend with the granny, who acquired a smattering of English when she was a "kitchen girl" in the suburbs. Casually they hi and what's-up die arme ouma who is startled by their very English English. "Oh granny, you're so stupid!" Holy Moses — in Africa nogal! But you ain't seen nothing yet, mtshana.

In a room full of extended family — shabbily dressed uncles, aunts and oumas — the youngsters swagger contemptuously among the riffraff. Shamed and aggrieved, their fatcat parents fumble for words as they berate their brood for not greeting their elderly relatives. But their now Anglicised brood angrily retort: "But folks, why should we greet strangers?" Laf'elihle kakhulu madoda! Cry the beloved country! But there's more …

While appeasing the ancestors there's ululating and praise-singing as the rustic uncles butcher the sacrificial cow, but the detribalised kids are horrified. "But that's barbaric … that's cruelty to animals!" they shrill. "Honey, that's for the ancestors. Your uncle had to do it and that's why I'm a bit short of cash this month. They are my family so I had to chip in and help him," whispers the embarrassed dad to his youngest child.

"What? Why didn't he budget for it?" the oldest child asks. "But he's family; it's the custom that I should help," dad points out weakly. "I wouldn't give him a cent! Just because we share a surname doesn't entitle him to our hard-earned money," sneers the teenager as the blushing dad and perplexed relatives look on, mtshana.

"For your information, young lady, you'll be obliged to help with household money this month because I forked out plenty for your uncle to organise the ancestral ceremony," says the fatcat dad to his eldest daughter.

"Damn your brother and his stupid amadlozi ceremony, daddy," the daughter whines. "You won't see a cent of my money! If you and your brother don't know how to budget, then hard luck!" she adds. "Ouch! That hurts," the poor ancestors wince in their graves. Tyini, unzima lomthwalo. Good old ancient Africa – where are you?

Joe Khumalo

112 PACE March 1997

FIGURE 3.8 Joe's Beat

This article was published in 1999. How does it position foreigners and locals? How does Khumalo use his multilingual resources to do this? What is the relevance of this text today? Is his use of an African township variety of English appropriate here? There are translations in the notes of the words Joe uses; look at these after you have done the work on the next page.[8]

MULTILINGUALISM—MIXIN', SWITCHIN' AND BORROWIN'

MULTILINGUALISM

When most colonised countries achieved independence in the years after World War II they had to decide what their official language would be. Many of them kept the language of the country that colonised them. They had been influenced by Western thinking that one language was an important part of building a nation. This one-nation-one-language thinking came from countries where monolingualism was the norm. The reality is that the world is multilingual not monolingual. This is particularly true for people in Africa.

Multilingual people have a repertoire of different languages and different varieties. Sometimes these are equally well developed. More often each language has been developed in relation to a specific need or limited purpose. Their ability to speak more than one language is an asset. It enhances mobility and contact with other people. It also provides insight into other cultures because of the way different languages construct the world differently.

Often people with multilingual repertoires harness their range of language resources for communication. When a person begins to talk in one language and then switches to another we call this *code-switching*. Often speakers are not even aware that they have switched. *Code-mixing* is when speakers use words or phrases from different languages in their sentences. When we have access to other languages we often *borrow* words to use in our own language. These words become part of our language and we forget where they originally come from.

Languages express the ideas and experiences of a group of people. They are influenced by a group's history, culture and values. This means it can be difficult to translate words and concepts exactly from one language to the next. Not all words exist in all languages. For example: *saudade* (Portuguese) has no English equivalent. It can be described in English as the special feeling one has of missing a person who has gone.

Ilunga (Thiluba, spoken in Zaire) means where a person will forgive any abuse the first time, tolerate it the second time but not the third time.

What other words do you know that do not have an equivalent in English?

English has borrowed words from lots of languages. Which languages did these words originally come from?

aardvark	bungalow	chocolate	economy
ghoul	gimmick	ignoramus	mosquito
parachute	saga	tycoon	zombie

FIGURE 3.9 Chart[9]

Discuss this question

Can you write a multilingual text even if your readers do not speak/read all your languages? Then read the article on the previous page by Joe Khumalo (Figure 3.8). He is a columnist for a local South African magazine, *Pace*.

1. In light of your discussion how successful do you think Khumalo has been? Do you need to know all the words to understand this article? Why/Why not? How does he balance his use of English and other languages? To what effect?
2. Rewrite the article in Standard English. Then compare it with the original. What are the strengths and the weaknesses of each version?
3. Find other examples in local texts you have read where writers use different language varieties and/or code-switch.

LINGUISTIC REPERTOIRES

One should not assume that multilingualism necessarily makes people more powerful. Blommaert makes the point that we all have 'truncated' repertoires—a range of specific competences in different languages, some highly developed and others less developed. There are also always resources that we lack.

Consider the language repertoires of Julien and Jan and take a position in relation to what you imagine to be their

- life histories
- potential mobility (where they can move to)
- social status and prestige locally and internationally
- economic power locally and internationally
- access to opportunity.

Justify your position based on what you have learned about language and power. You could also include considerations of history and geography. Julien lives in the Democratic Republic of Congo, once a Belgian colony. Jan was born in Belgium. Belgium is closer to the centre of world power. Africa is on the periphery, at the margins.

Jan

Jan is multilingual and has competence in four languages: Dutch, French, German and English. Dutch is his home language. He can use vernacular dialects and the standard variety of Dutch and he can produce complex formal writing in this language. He learnt French in school and on the streets of Brussels. He is more fluent in Flemish-Brussels vernacular French than in standard French. He can read French well but is less competent in writing. Giving formal talks in French is beyond his ability. He learnt German at school. He learnt English last but does all his professional work in English. He has a highly developed literacy in English and has worked as a professional in London, but has very little ability in vernacular forms of English. He also studied Swahili and knows it well enough to translate documents written in Swahili.

(Based on Blommaert 2010, *The Sociolinguistics of Globalisation*, pp. 103–105)

Julien

Julien is likely to have varying degrees of competence in Shaba-Swahili varieties, local vernacular French, probably one or more Luba-languages . . . and given the dominance of that language in the Mobutu era in the Congo also some proficiency in Lingala. We have evidence of writing skills in Shaba-Swahili and French but not in the other languages. When Julien travels to Lubumbashi, he is likely to use Shaba-Swahili; when he travels to Mbuji-Mayi, he finds himself in a Luba speaking environment. When he visits Belgian missionaries he would probably speak French, Luba and/or Shaba-Swahili. Since he married a woman in Kinshasa, some Lingala could be part of the family code, although the area where he locates his family would be Luba and Swahili speaking. Code-switching would be the rule rather than the exception.

(Blommaert 2008, *Grassroots Literacy*, p. 35)

Jan Blommaert looks at the ways in which globalisation is affecting language. He looks at how you can learn to speak with an American accent over the internet, so that you can get a job in a call centre. In this case, the accent you acquire is de-linked from place. You can be anywhere in the world and still sound as if you are in America. He is interested in studying how languages work as signifying resources in a globalised world and how they produce differential access and inequality.

THE DOMINANCE OF ENGLISH

FIGURE 3.10

English: the world's biggest brand

How did English become a powerful language? Is it the most powerful language in the world?

Can English remain powerful? What other languages might take its place in the future?

English is constructed here as a commodity. What is the effect of viewing English in this way?

Who sells the product? Who is buying it? Why is English desirable?

If English is the biggest global brand find out how much money it makes.

Linguistic Imperialism is a term used to describe the process of imposing and maintaining the dominance of English. And in doing so how does it create structural and cultural inequalities between English and other languages? How can branding English be seen as an act of linguistic imperialism?

Read the extract from a speech made in 2008 by ex-British Prime Minister Gordon Brown. How is Britain positioned here? How is the rest of the world positioned? What will Britain gain and what will countries who take up his offer gain? What might the losses be? Is this an example of linguistic imperialism?

> The English language, like football and other sports, began here and has spread to every corner of the globe. Today more than a billion people speak English. But there are millions of people in every continent who are still denied this chance to learn English. And I believe that no one—however poor, however distant—should be denied the opportunity that the English language provides. So I want Britain to make a new gift to the world—pledging to help and support anyone, whatever their circumstances, to have access to the tools they need to learn or to teach English. And my plan is that in the next 10 years at least 1 billion more people in the villages, towns and cities of every continent will have access to resources, materials and qualifications from the UK. . . . And we will work with . . . providers of English language training to raise the number of programmes on the English curriculum accessible via the web. . . . This is a great opportunity for Britain—and a measure of the greatness that lies not in empire or territory but through a language that has the power to bring this world of over 200 countries together. We will take up with vigour the bold task of making our language the world's common language of choice.
>
> (Adapted from speech transcript found at www.number10.gov.uk)

I WANT YOU TO LEARN ENGLISH

FIGURE 3.11 I want you to learn English

And on the other side of the Atlantic the English Only Movement uses national symbols to show intolerance. Find out how they do this.

A THREAT TO OTHER LANGUAGES?

WHO SPEAKS ENGLISH?

The dominant group of English speakers in the world do not speak English as their home language. Speakers of English may speak it as their second language, as a foreign language, or use it as a *lingua franca*. A *lingua franca* is a language used to communicate between speakers who have different mother tongues.

What other languages are used as *lingua francas*?

DISCUSS

1. What are the advantages of speaking English?

2. What does English give people access to?

3. One of the consequences of choosing one language over another is the potential loss of the mother tongue or home language. Why is this a loss?

4. How can local people and governments make sure that people have access to learning and using a dominant language and still maintain their mother tongue or home languages?

FIGURE 3.12
Language death

If language and culture are so closely tied together is it possible to express who you are, your culture, community ways of knowing and being in the world if you have to do it in another language? What happens if you did not choose this language but were forced to learn it? Two famous African writers have two very different positions on this issue. Read up on their positions and decide which one you agree with.

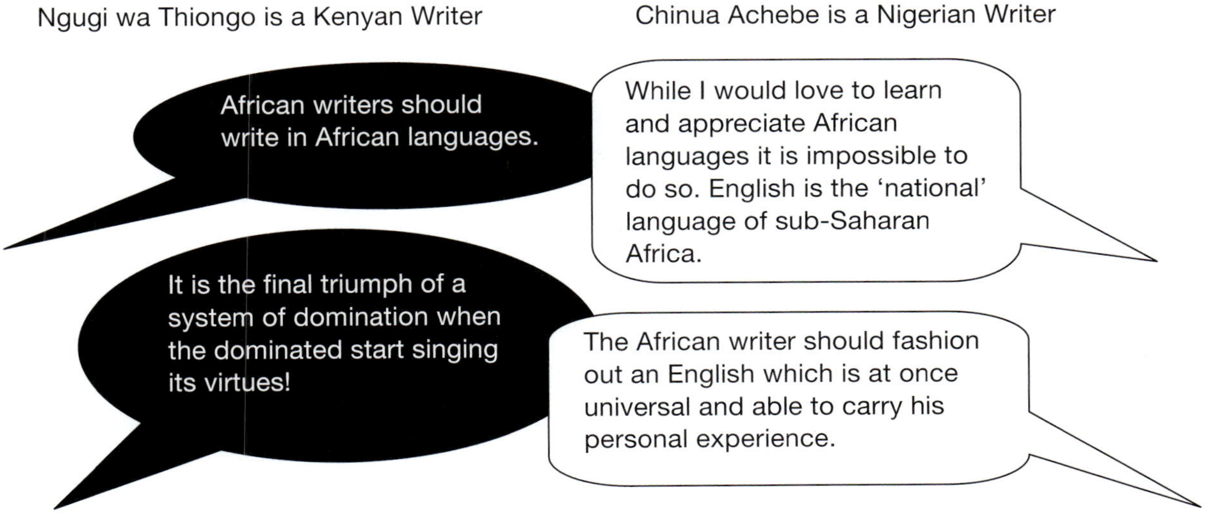

Ngugi wa Thiongo is a Kenyan Writer

Chinua Achebe is a Nigerian Writer

African writers should write in African languages.

While I would love to learn and appreciate African languages it is impossible to do so. English is the 'national' language of sub-Saharan Africa.

It is the final triumph of a system of domination when the dominated start singing its virtues!

The African writer should fashion out an English which is at once universal and able to carry his personal experience.

FIGURE 3.13 African writers' views on English

APPROPRIATING ENGLISH

It is not just writers who appropriate (take and make their own) English. Ordinary people do this too. Jennifer Jenkins talks about two groups of non-native English speakers (NNS). The first group mostly need to communicate with native speakers of English. They are likely to learn a standard form of English to make themselves understood. The second group will mostly communicate with other non-native speakers in English. It is the second group who are changing English because they are developing their own ways of communicating with each other to meet their specific communication needs. No longer are grammar and correctness the most important part of communicating. What is important is that the message is intelligible. Speakers draw on their knowledge of languages, cultures and contexts to use English in innovative ways. Saying 'He got his informations, isn't it?' or 'I want that we go now' is not incorrect in contexts where NNS get their message across to other NNS.

FIGURE 3.14 Hakuna kazi bila

Source: *Sunday Standard*, Kenya.

This is taken from a Kenyan newspaper.

Can you find examples of other texts where a new variety of English is being used in local contexts? Try to find visual examples, song lyrics, published fiction, and samples of speech.

Bring these to share with your class. What is English being used for? Who are the speakers and the audience? How is English is being used?

These new varieties are being called World Englishes.

1. How does the meaning of English change in the plural form?
2. What challenges will World Englishes present for teachers of English?
3. How does this shift power relations?
4. What changes to their thinking about language might native speakers have to make?
5. What will happen to the old rules for Standard English?
6. Who do you think will make the new rules?
7. What do you think the dominant variety of English will be in 2040?

Some people see English as a killer language that will lead to the death of other languages. What do you think? To put the question more concretely: If millions of Mandarin or isiZulu speakers learn English, will Mandarin or isiZulu die?

Section 4: Grammar as a resource for critical literacy

This is one of three sections that provides tools for analyzing texts. Here the focus is on the choice of the verbal signs and their effects. The signs discussed here are based on Michael Halliday's grammar. This is a functional grammar that focuses on how grammatical choices encode three kinds of meaning in every clause. Halliday calls these functions. It is of course not possible to work with the complete grammar, so I have chosen those aspects of the grammar that are key for constructing and interpreting positions in texts.

Ideational function (ideas)

Halliday's ideational function gives us the content of the clause. It tells us who is doing what to whom in what circumstances. It is important to remember that the doer and the done-to need not be live participants as in 'The car ran out of gas'. Other grammars talk about subjects and objects of the verb. Halliday describes these as participants (*doers* and *done-tos*, see page 78) and processes (p. 78). He prefers the term processes to make us aware of different kinds of actions.

TABLE 4.1 Processes

Process	Explanation	Examples
Doing	Acting in/on the world	Play, show, run, take
Feeling Thinking Sensing	The 'actions' are mental—inside the head	Love, envy. Imagine, believe. See, hear, smell
Having	I have a car—relations of possession	Have, own, possess
Being	I am a student—relations of identity	Am, are, is
Saying	Introduce what is said	Declare, report, mutter

Which participants are constructed with which processes is often very telling. Imagine one participant who is a doer—gets things done—and another who is a sayer—all talk and no action. These are very different representations. It also matters whether one acts (doer) or is passively acted upon (done-to).

Page 72 deals with how participants are named and page 73 with how processes are turned into participants. Pages 74 and 75 examine the use of pronouns. Circumstances are not dealt with here.

Interpersonal function (relationships)

Two aspects of the interpersonal function are dealt with—mood (p. 77) and modality (p. 80).

I will use Section 4 to illustrate the effect of the choice of *mood*. *This* page is full of statements that construct you as needing the information that I have to give. In the introduction to activities, I use commands (listen, p. 71; examine, p. 72; practise, p. 73; investigate, p. 75 and so on). Do I have the right to do this? If so, what gives me the right? What rights do you have? I have just asked a whole lot of questions. What effect does this have? How does this differ from the use of questions on page 76? The explanation of mood on page 77 shows how the choice constructs either the speaker or the listener as having something that the other one needs. This can indicate differences in power and access.

Modality (p. 80) on the other hand works with degrees of certainty and authority and it is different from tense. Tense is a claim to truth. The statement, 'Hilary Janks wrote a book called *Literacy and Power*' uses the past tense to make a categorical statement. If a statement is categorical it can be shown to be true or not. By way of contrast the statement 'Hilary Janks *may* have written *Literacy and Power*' uses modality to show a lack of certainty. This is not a truth claim but a statement of possibility.

Textual function (organization)

This function has to do with how the words are arranged to form a clause. What comes first? What comes last? What is emphasized? How? It is also concerned with how clauses are linked to other clauses to construct a text.

How the text sticks together or is cohesive is the subject of p. 82. You are asked to look for repetitions, synonyms, pronouns that tie the text together. How the article is used (p. 75) is also an aspect of *cohesion*. Three kinds of cohesion are shown in Table 4.2.

The starting point of the clause, what

TABLE 4.2 Cohesion

Cohesion	Explanation	Examples
Reference	Refers back over short stretches of text	Pronouns. The definite article refers to what is known
Lexical cohesion	Connects words by repetition, synonyms, antonyms over long stretches of text	Husband, wife, couple, family, children, home, marriage, love, divorce—are all connected
Conjunction	Joins clauses and sets up logical relations	Because—reason. If—condition When—time

Halliday calls *theme*, can be examined in a text to see what is foregrounded. The theme is the launch pad for the idea in the clause and it gives us a sense of the concerns of the clause and, if these are patterned, of the text. Halliday also looks at how focus is brought to information. In spoken texts we do this with our voice and in written texts

BY CHANGING THE FONT in some way. This makes some words jump out. Theme and *information focus* are the subject of page 83.

A multifunctional grammar

What is brilliant about Halliday's grammar is that it works for both speech and writing, and it operates in every clause and therefore throughout a text. Every clause has to have participants and processes, processes have to have tense or modality, something has to come first and last, and every clause is structured as a statement, question or command.

What we have to consider is the effects of how participants are named and attached to particular processes, the effects of tense or of modality, the effects of foregrounding, backgrounding and cohesion.

Power, diversity, access and design

Knowledge of the grammar helps you know where to look in order to understand how language choices work in relation to power, identity/difference and access. The emphasis in this section, however, is on design. Texts are designed by the choices that are made. Different choices are needed for redesign.

Halliday is a linguist who helps us to understand that when we use language we choose from a range of options and from a range of ways of combining the choices we make. Depending on what we choose, we realize the potential that language offers us in different ways. Because writers and speakers make choices when they use language, texts are never neutral—they are always positioned and they work to position readers. The same is true of images. In the next few pages the focus will be on grammar—the ways in which English allows us to select and to combine sounds into words, words into sentences and sentences into texts.

THE GRAMMAR OF SOUND

When we use language we create meaning by the choices and combinations that we make. It is important to remember that every choice we make affects meaning. This is how we 'realise' the potential of language in one way rather than another. Here we focus on choice in relation to the sound system of English.

> **SOUNDS INTO WORDS**
>
> Different languages use sounds in different ways. Chinese for instance does not have an *r* sound, which is why Chinese speakers substitute an *l* sound for *r* when they speak English. African languages only have five vowel sounds, which is why they often do not make a distinction between words like *ship* and *sheep*, *counsel* and *cancel.* If your language does not have a sound, then it is hard to hear these sounds in another language and even harder to say them. So, for instance, English speakers cannot hear the differences in the Chinese pronunciation of the word *ma*, which, depending on the tone used, can mean five different things. Tone refers to whether the word is pronounced with a rising or falling intonation or a mixture of rising and falling. African languages are also tonal. In addition, they have click sounds and aspirated sounds that English speakers struggle to pronounce.

1. Our attitudes to others are often based on their accents. Give examples.

2. How do our attitudes create power differences and affect people's sense of identity?

FIGURE 4.1 Pronunciation

Listen to movies with a critical ear for accents: Are accents used to include or exclude?

1. Return to the discussion of the baddies in Hollywood movies.
2. Describe the accents of the good guys and the bad guys. What effects do these choices have?
3. Consider the accents given to animals in specific animated movies that you have seen? What do the accents make us feel about the characters?
4. Consider the accents given to characters in kiddies' television. Why were these accents chosen? What effects do they have?

NAMING

Critical readers and writers pay attention to words. The words we choose to name our experiences construct particular versions of events. It is the naming that shows our positions. As speakers and writers we want people to believe us, to agree with us and to support us. We use words to achieve this.

Wording constructs the world.

- Lexis is the technical term for the words in a language (words).
- To lexicalise is to put something into words (to choose words).
- Lexicalization is the end result of the word choices made (the wording).

The words of the language offer us potential ways of making meaning. We choose from this potential when we lexicalize. The lexicalization is the end result—the realization of language's meaning potential.

HSBC is an International Investment Bank. In its advertising, it represents itself as open to the diverse views and needs of its clients. To do so, it created several series of beautiful images that had contradictory interpretations depending on the viewer's point of view. Many of these advertisements can be seen by googling 'HSBC advertising' in Google Images. We designed the images below to give you a good idea of how the HSBC advertisements work. The HSBC billboard-size advertisements were displayed in international airports. How do the labels force you to re-read the image?

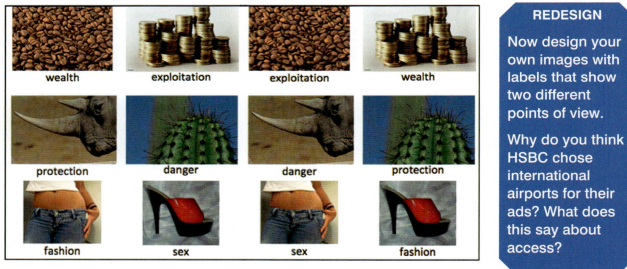

FIGURE 4.2 Made-up example of ads similar to HSBC advertisements

REDESIGN

Now design your own images with labels that show two different points of view.

Why do you think HSBC chose international airports for their ads? What does this say about access?

Examine the words below that have been used in reports on the internet to describe the killers and the event that took place at Columbine high school. Discuss their positioning effects.

Killers, murderers, kids with serious psychological problems, senior high school students, victims of bullying, teenagers, loners, terrorists, shooters.	Killing, deadliest high school massacre, grand terrorist bombing, shooting, an all-out assault on Columbine, the Columbine massacre, Columbine.

See page 63 and http://history1900s.about.com/od/famouscrimesscandals/a/columbine_3.htm

NOMINALISATION OR NOUNING

Instead of using a verb to construct an action, we can choose to turn the verb into a noun. Halliday calls this nominalization. I call this *nouning* the verb. Nouning turns actions into things. It focuses on the end result of the action, the state of affairs produced by the action.

Two examples of nouning:

1. Shoppers consume (verb) goods.
   The economy depends on consumerism (noun).

2. Russia invaded (verb) Georgia.
   The invasion (noun) of Georgia was a threat to peace.

> Verbs have
> - *subjects* who do the action (shoppers, Russia)
> - *tense*, which tells you the time and frequency of the action (buy, invaded)
> - *modality*, which tells you about certainty or uncertainty (invaded/may have invaded)
>
> Nouns have none of these.

The Columbine High School **massacre** <u>occurred</u> on Tuesday, April 20, 1999, at Columbine High School in the United States. Two senior students, Eric Harris and Dylan Klebold, <u>embarked</u> on a **massacre.** 12 students and one teacher <u>were killed</u>. 21 other students <u>were injured</u>. The pair then <u>committed</u> **suicide**. It is the deadliest high **school massacre** in United States **history**. The **massacre** <u>provoked</u> **debate** regarding gun **control** laws, the **availability** of firearms in the United States, and gun **violence** involving youths. Much **discussion** also <u>centered</u> on the nature of high school cliques, subcultures and **bullying**, as well as the **role** of violent movies and video games in American society. The **shooting** also <u>resulted</u> in an increased **emphasis** on school **security**, and a moral **panic** <u>aimed</u> at goth culture, social outcasts, and the **use** of pharmaceutical anti-depressants by teenagers.

(Adapted from Wikipedia)

> Nominalizations are in bold. Verbs have been underlined.
>
> 1. What are the effects of nouning?
> 2. How much action is there in the verbs that are left?
> 3. Rewrite the passage converting the nouns into verbs.
> 4. What is the effect of the use of the passive voice in *were killed* and *were injured*?

Practise nouning the verbs in a different account of Columbine

Ten years have passed since Harris and Klebold made Columbine a synonym for rage. New information indicates that much of what the public has been told about what they did is wrong. They planned their crime in cold blood. They saved money from after-school jobs, took Advanced Placement classes, assembled a small arsenal and fooled everyone. They intended to commit suicide only after they had terrorized and killed more people than at Oklahoma City. If they hadn't wired the timers so badly, the propane bombs they set to go off in the cafeteria would have wiped out 600 people. After those bombs exploded, they planned to gun down fleeing survivors. They had packed their cars with bombs to rip through still more crowds, presumably of survivors, rescue workers, and reporters.

(Adapted from www.usatoday.com and www.slade.com)

PRONOUNS

Who are 'we' and who are 'they'? Inclusive and exclusive pronouns

Pronouns stand in for nouns. The pronouns (I, you, he/she, we, you and they) together with the possessive pronouns (my, your, his/her, our and their) often show us who is *included* and who is excluded.

Read the following advertisement from the United Nations High Commission for Refugees (UNHCR) and underline every pronoun and every possessive pronoun. In each case work out what noun each pronoun is standing in for. Once you have done this, work out who is 'we' and who is 'they' in this text.

1. Describe people who are the same as you.
2. Describe people who are different from you.
3. Why does the UNHCR want us to believe that all people are the same?
4. What is the effect of using *he* for the refugee? Do a gender analysis of the Lego dolls.
5. What are the effects of using Lego people in rows?

FIGURE 4.3 Top half of UNHCR advertisement

FIGURE 4.4 Bottom half of UNHCR advertisement

SPOT THE REFUGEE

There he is. Fourth row, second from the left. The one with the moustache. Obvious really.

Maybe not. The unsavoury-looking character you're looking at is more likely to be your average neighbourhood slob with a grubby vest and a weekend's stubble on his chin.

And the real refugee could just as easily be the clean-cut fellow on his left.

You see, refugees are just like you and me.

Except for one thing.

Everything they once had has been left behind. Home, family, possessions, all gone. They have nothing.

And nothing is all they'll ever have unless we all extend a helping hand.

We know you can't give them back the things that others have taken away.

We're not even asking for money (though every penny certainly helps).

But we are asking that you keep an open mind. And a smile of welcome.

It may not seem much. But to a refugee it can mean everything.

UNHCR is a strictly humanitarian organization funded only by voluntary contributions. Currently it is responsible for more than 19 million refugees around the world.

UNHCR Public Information
P.O. Box 2500
1211 Geneva 2, Switzerland

Newsweek

United Nations High Commissioner for Refugees

Models courtesy of The LEGO Group.

Us/them language

Look out for us/them language. It is a sure sign that the not-us people are being spoken about negatively. In Thompson's terms it is the language used to divide. It is often racist or sexist or homophobic. It is often used to make the Other look bad.

PRONOUNS

He/she language

In the 1980s feminist linguists argued that the conventional use of English was sexist. At the time, *he* or *man* were used to stand for people in general. *He* could include she, but *she* could not be used to include men. This was passed as an Act of Parliament in the United Kingdom in 1850. Feminist linguists argued that this man-made language constructed women as inferior and made them invisible. They tried to invent a gender-neutral pronoun but were not successful. They did, however, manage to change the convention. These days people use *he or she* or sometimes *s/he*. Sometimes *they* is used as a singular gender-neutral pronoun. Sexist language is language that privileges men at the expense of women.

RESEARCH PROJECT

Investigate the work of the feminist linguists. What other aspects of language did they see as man-made? Looking back several decades later assess what they did and did not manage to achieve. You could start with the work of Dale Spender, Deborah Cameron and Deborah Tannen.

FIGURE 4.5
Gender neutral

The article

English has a definite (*the*) and an indefinite article (*a* or *an*). What this implies is that when we use *the* the reader knows what we are referring to. This is what makes it definite. The statement 'They need to catch the poachers and give them extended sentences' assumes that the reader knows which poachers the writer is talking about. The use of *the* positions the listener/reader as someone who knows and reveals the assumptions of the writer or the speaker.

RHINO POACHING CRISIS IN SOUTH AFRICA

200 rhinos have been killed in *the* last six months. Poachers shoot *the* rhinos and chop off their horns using an axe or a panga.

The demand for rhino horn in Asia, where it is used for traditional medicine, is driving poaching in Africa.

Conservationists want to see international moves to crack down on *the* supply and demand ends of the chain in order to save *the* rhino.

But WWF is warning *the* problem could be spreading, as Swaziland reported its first loss of a rhino to poaching for 20 years.

> Analyse every use of *the*.

FIGURE 4.6 Rhino

WHO SPEAKS?

Critical questions for interaction

- Who gets to speak?
- How often do people speak?
- Who is silent/silenced?
- Who speaks for whom?
- Who interrupts?
- Who gets heard?
- Who controls the topic?
- Whose points are followed through?
- Whose rules for turn-taking are used?

Critical questions for reported speech

- Who gets reported in direct speech?
- Who gets reported in indirect speech?
- Who gets quoted first?
- Who gets quoted last?
- Who gets quoted the most?
- How does the reporting word position the speech?
- What belongs to the speaker and what belongs to the reporter?
- Is it possible that someone was misquoted or quoted selectively?
- Is it possible that the person was quoted out of context?

Reporting verbs frame speech positively or negatively.

announced; affirmed; asserted; alleged; avowed; claimed; disclosed; divulged; contended; exclaimed; expressed; hinted; insisted; maintained; muttered; mumbled; pronounced; stated; stammered; swore; uttered; whined; whispered.

Find others.

FIGURE 4.7 Reporting verbs

Use these questions to analyse this and other texts that report speech

Why are there no inverted commas?

What effect is created by this reporting verb?

Is this a quote or a headline?

How is reporting used to position the people who came to see the mermaid?

Is there evidence that the reporter witnessed the event?

Who did the reporter interview? Did he speak to the visitors?

What reports are there by people not connected with the aquarium? Does this matter?

She's no mermaid cry visitors to the aquarium

Lorelei the mermaid caused an uproar at the East London beachfront when she was pelted with soft-drink cans by visitors demanding a refund from the city's aquarium because she was not real.

Between 300 and 400 people flocked to the aquarium to see to see the mythical sea creature during the hour she was on show on Friday. The mermaid was in fact a publicity stunt in the form of 18-year-old Tessa du Toit, who had been working as a guide at the aquarium.

"Most people who came knew there was no such thing as a mermaid, but a few who truly believed in it got a bit out of hand when the discovered the truth," she said.

Some members of the public were so upset that they started hurling their soft-drink cans at her and hurling verbal abuse.

Some of the crowd realised Lorelei was a fake only when she refused to swim because it would ruin the specially made mermaid outfit.

Aquarium curator Willie Maritz said the aquarium had been accused of trying to steal the public's money when in fact it was only trying to help the city by attracting people to the aquarium.

Tourism East London director Crain Nancarrow, who came up with the mermaid ploy said, "I thought it was a well known fact that mermaids don't exist. This was purely a publicity stunt to put East London on the map and, as far as I'm concerned, it worked."

He added: "We underestimated the response we would get from the public, but we take this as a learning experience and we also now realise the power of the media."

Due to the bad crowd behavior, Maritz has decided not to show the mermaid again.
Sapa

FIGURE 4.8 She's no mermaid . . .

STATEMENTS, QUESTIONS, COMMANDS AND OFFERS

These are the four moods for clauses in English and each works to position the listener differently.

Mood	Speaker	Possible positions for the listener to take up
Statement	Gives information	The listener needs the information. Listeners can accept or reject it.
Question	Asks for information	The listener is someone who knows the answer. S/he can give the information or refuse to share it.
Command	Demands goods or services	The listener is someone that the speaker has the right to command. The speaker can obey or disobey the command.
Offer	Offers goods or services	The listener can accept or reject the offer.

How does the choice of mood construct the reader in this AIDS awareness advertisement?

Work out the mode for each clause in the text below. Look for the patterns and explain their effects. Each clause has one finite verb.

Who, in their right frame of mind, would sacrifice their whole life for more feeling?

Isn't that the argument? How can you eat a sweet while it is still in its wrapper? How can you take a shower with a raincoat on? It sounds intelligent, doesn't it? The truth of the matter is that when it comes to eating sweets, you are in no danger of dying. And unless some freak accident occurs, you are not going to die having a shower either.

But with sex the stakes are higher. You could lose your life. So make an informed choice now. What is important to you? Is it your life and the bright future that this country of ours has on offer or is it more feeling for that hour or so that you spend having sex?

Think about it. And, don't rush. When you have come to an informed decision, act sensibly because aside from abstinence or both of you being faithful to each other, condoms are the only other way to stop the spread of the incurable disease that is HIV. The virus that eventually causes AIDS.

Call your local clinic to find out where to get condoms. Get the condoms and use them. Always. And promise never to discriminate against people living with HIV/AIDS. Instead, show them some support by wearing a red ribbon. If the above sounds familiar to you and you are practising it, welcome to the red ribbon family. And tell the rest of the world it's ok to feel a little less as long as it guarantees you a much longer life.

FIGURE 4.9 AIDS Advertisement

DOINGS, DOERS AND DONE-TOS

Words combine to form clauses. Every clause tells us who is doing what and they often tell us who they are doing it to. So clauses have doers and done-tos. Doers usually have more power than done-tos. For example: *The boys beat the girls* means something very different from *The girls beat the boys*.

DOERS AND DONE-TOS HAVE DIFFERENT NAMES IN DIFFERENT GRAMMARS		
Doers	**Done-tos**	
Subject	Verbs	Object
Participant	Processes: These are not just about doing . They also tell us about thinking or feeling (a mental process), saying (verbal processes), being or having (relational), and behaving.	Participant
Agent/actor	Actions	Acted on

In the following clauses, who is the doer and who is the done-to? Notice that:

- In active voice the doer is in the first part of the sentence and the done-to in the last part.
- In passive voice the done-to comes first and the doer comes last. **FIGURE 4.10** Cat and mouse
- In the passive voice you can leave the doer out altogether.

Active voice	**Passive voice**	**Passive voice**
The dog ate the cat.	The cat was eaten by the dog.	The cat was eaten.
The cat ate the mouse.	The mouse was eaten by the cat.	The mouse was eaten.
The mouse ate the cheese.	The cheese was eaten by the mouse.	The cheese was eaten.

In addition to who is the doer and how many actions are given to each doer, it makes a difference what kind of doing is given to each of the actors. What kind of doing has been chosen for each clause? In which of these has the homework been done?

Kabelo did his homework. Kabelo hated his homework. He talked about his homework. He thought about his homework. The homework is not a problem.

Read 'Egg and Sperm Race' (Figure 4.12). Find all the processes. Answer the critical questions.

How is the sperm positioned? How is the egg positioned? Do the text and the cartoon match the headline?

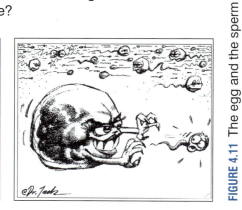

FIGURE 4.11 The egg and the sperm

CRITICAL QUESTIONS TO ASK ABOUT VERBS/PROCESSES

Are the actions positive or negative ?	Who is the done-to ?	Who is the doer ?	Who is given the most to do ?	Who does? Who says? Who thinks/ feels? Who has what? Who is what? ?

TECHNOLOGY
Egg and sperm race—who's the runner?

Rob Stepney in London

Conventional descriptions of sperm as active, and eggs as passive, participants in fertilisation owe more to gender stereotypes than to true facts of life.

Given the evidence about how sperm and egg really perform it is time we replaced the dead hand of sexist metaphor with something more appropriate.

This at least is the thesis advanced by professor Emily Martin, of the anthropology department in Johns Hopkins University, Baltimore, in the latest issue of the gynaecology journal *Orgyn*.

The standard story runs something like this: having battled its way against overwhelming odds from the vagina to the oviduct, a single valiant sperm succeeds in penetrating the egg, so fertilising it and engendering new life. In contrast to this heroic endeavour, the egg is shed by the ovary and swept down the fallopian tube to await its date with destiny. For years I have used similar vocabulary in writing about reproduction.

So have many others. A delve into a biology textbook, chosen at random, shows that the sperms' efforts to reach the egg are indeed emphasised: the difficulty of their journey is likened to a man swimming in an Atlantic Ocean of treacle.

In the process of fertilisation, the sperm is also described as the dominant partner, releasing enzymes that dissolve the outer coat of the egg and producing a filament to pierce its membrane.

But at least this is less aggressive vocabulary than that used in a paper cited by Emily Martin, which has the egg being harpooned by the sperm. She also reproduces a cartoon from *Science News* showing sperm attacking the egg with a jackhammer and pickaxe. Such images project cultural values on to the 'personalities' of sex cells, she says.

The biological reality, she argues, is entirely different. According to recent research by biophysicists at Johns Hopkins University, sperm rather than propelling themselves manfully onwards, are ditherers. 'The motion of the sperm's tail makes the head move sideways with a force that is 10 times stronger than its forward movement', Martin reports.

Instead of coming equipped to penetrate, it seems that sperm are designed to avoid attachment —a feature which makes sense given that they are far more likely to encounter cells that are not eggs than they are to meet the ovum.

It therefore falls to the egg to perform the crucial role of cementing the relationship. The ovum's adhesive surface traps the sperm, which is left wiggling ineffectually until the genetic material in its head is engulfed by the egg.

But Martin argues, to describe the events in these terms may simply be to replace one damaging metaphor with another. Instead of sperm as Superman, we have egg as some kind of predatory spider. The most appropriate model, she suggests, is to regard sperm and egg as mutually dependent agents interacting to achieve a common goal.

Instead of active and passive, we have 'feedback loops' and 'flexible adaptation'. This seems appropriate given evidence that molecules on the sperm and the ovum have equal roles in enabling male and female genes to come together.

We are familiar with such ideas of interplay and self-regulation when it comes to biological processes such as the hormonal system. No-one can be sure of how powerfully biological metaphors reinforce social stereotypes, or vice versa.

But we should perhaps now be seeing the conjunction of sperm and egg in terms that do more than simply echo outdated gender roles.

FIGURE 4.12 Egg and sperm race

Investigation of other media representations of gender

Find examples of women as doers. What are they doing?
Find examples of women as done-tos. Who are they done to by?
Find examples of men as doers. What are they doing?
Find examples of men as done-tos. Who are they done to by?

Does your investigation confirm or refute the active passive binary discussed on page 48?

CERTAINTY AND UNCERTAINTY

Tense is used to express categorical truth (*it is*/*it isn't* or *do it*/*don't do it*).

Modality is used to express degrees of certainty and uncertainty (*must, will, may*) in relation to how probable or usual statements are. It also shows how obliged or inclined one is to obey commands or to offer goods or services.

Study the use of modality in claims about global warming.

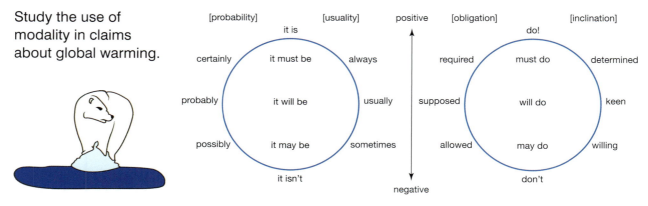

FIGURE 4.14 Modality chart

FIGURE 4.13
Diminishing icebergs

Authority

Modality also shows how confident one is about something. People who have a great deal of knowledge can speak with great certainty and authority. Find examples in this workbook of authoritative writing. People can also pretend to know more than they do. Modality is a powerful resource for positioning people and information.

Read the dialogue below and discuss the use of tense and modality.

Pinky   Do you think you could do the dishes and clean the house today?

Sue   Not really. Might you be able to help out as I think I have a full schedule.

Pinky   What do you mean by 'you think'? Do you or don't you? Surely you know.

Sue   Either way, can it wait until tomorrow?

Pinky   Definitely not. It's your turn and you always procrastinate. Why should I have to wait for you to do your share of the work? I am tired of living in a pig sty.

Sue   OK. I'll try to find time later.

Pinky   You must make the time or I will have to find a different house-mate to share with.

Find an example of a political speech and explain where there is certainty and where there is uncertainty as well as how you know.

Who made this speech? When?

'YES WE CAN
TO JUSTICE AND EQUALITY
TO OPPORTUNITY AND PROSPERITY
HEAL THIS NATION
REPAIR THIS WORLD
YES WE CAN.'

FOREGROUNDING AND BACKGROUNDING

If something has been backgrounded then it is not in the forefront of our minds. Foregrounding is a metaphor for ways in which text producers make ideas come to the front where we notice them more. Language has a number of resources for doing this. Most of them are resources for spoken language where it is easy to emphasize a word simply by changing our tone of voice. The equivalent in written text is italics or bold, or size of font or colour. Look at the different emphases in each of these sentences.

John washed the car yesterday.	John, not someone else, washed the car.
John *washed* the car yesterday.	John washed the car as opposed to driving it.
John washed *the car* yesterday.	It was the car that he washed, not the dog.
John washed the car *yesterday*.	He washed the car yesterday, not today.

Another resource for foregrounding is how we order the ideas in a clause. The technical term in Hallidayan grammar for the first bit of the clause before the verb is called the THEME. Because speakers and writers usually begin a thought with what is uppermost in their minds, the theme is the launch pad for the idea. Compare the same clause with different themes.

The resources for changing what is the focus of information are more economical than those of writing.

FIGURE 4.15
Launched

John washed the car yesterday. →	This is the standard participant-process-participant word order where the theme is old information and the part after the verb (the rheme) is new information.
Washing the car was what John did yesterday →	This unusual or marked (strange) word order puts the emphasis on the theme, washing the car.
The car was washed yesterday. →	Passive voice is the unmarked (normal) means of changing what is in theme position.
Yesterday John washed the car. →	Here time is in theme position.

But John washing the car is not that interesting. So look at foregrounding and backgrounding in the text below. See how the cars are positioned differently by what is in theme position in each clause. Once you have all the themes try to find patterns.

FIGURE 4.16
The *SL* guide to cars

REJOICE, ALL YE WHO KNOW NOTHING ABOUT CARS. YOUR DAYS OF PARKING-LOT SHAME ARE OVER. WE'VE ASKED THE WISEST AND MOST EXPERIENCED MOTORING JOURNALISTS OUT THERE TO DRIVE AND RATE PRETTY MUCH EVERY CAR ON THE MARKET, FROM CUTE LITTLE RUN-AROUNDS TO THE BIGGEST, BADDEST, SEXIEST MACHINES AVAILABLE. SO HERE IT IS, NO HOLDS BARRED:

SL magazine July 2004 p27 33
In this article each car was reviewed under four headings: Price, The Package, Street Cred and Verdict. Here only two sections for each car are included. These four cars were taken from the section on cars under R100 000.

the SL no bullsh*t guide to cars

CHEVROLET AVEO	DAIHATSU CHARADE	FORD FIESTA	CHEVROLET SPARK
STREET CRED The Aveo was released as a Daewoo in Europe. We won't tell anyone if you don't. If it had a V6 under the bonnet, you'd have a case, but right now, you'll have your work cut out to explain the road noise and those stylish hub-caps. **VERDICT** A sensible drive from A to B that won't let you down.	**STREET CRED** It may be small on the outside, but the Charade is big on the inside. Cram your mates in there and pull straws for the designated driver. Alloy wheels are included, which is impressive at this price. **VERDICT** Size counts, especially if you're a scrooge on the fuel bill.	**STREET CRED** You'll be the talk of the place in the three-door car. It has cutting-edge styling and the brilliance of Focus and Mondeo in a smaller package. Get away from their lame TV ad-campaign and you'll be onto a winner. **VERDICT** Fiesta really does mean party time.	**STREET CRED** One sheep in another sheep's clothing. Not a head-turner. **Verdict** Who's the bright Spark then?

82

HOLDING IT ALL TOGETHER

The linguistic glue that binds words to one another and clauses into texts is known as cohesion.

> We all know that conjunctions are 'joining' words; what we don't always recognize is that they also set up logical relations. Explain the different connections between cause and effect in the different versions of 'Veni. Vidi. Vici'.

> I came and I saw *and* I conquered.
> *Because* I came and saw, I conquered.
> I came in order to see, *so that* I could conquer.
> *When* I came, I saw and conquered.

In the following text find all the uses of pronouns, synonyms, antonyms and repetition that work to tie Pick 'n Pay to Mandela. On the text, you can even draw lines that connect them. The text is given below together with a small version of the original text. What is the genre of this text? What effect does the cohesion have?

FIGURE 4.17 Pick 'n Pay text

MADIBA
PLEASE ACCEPT THE FREEDOM OF PICK 'N PAY

We, the people of Pick 'n Pay, thank you for having 'made the difference' and wish you a long and happy retirement. Your long walk to freedom has been an inspiration to the world, to our beloved country, and to its people. Through your example, we see freedom as more than a release from physical bonds and oppression of human rights. We also see it as a release from bitterness and bigotry. You have fought for this country's freedom from ignorance and poverty and isolation. You have unlocked our hearts and minds, and opened the door to a brighter future. In appreciation, we hope that you will accept the key that is our symbolic gift of freedom—the Freedom of Pick 'n Pay. *It entitles you and your wife Graça, for the rest of your life, to shop for your groceries at any Pick 'n Pay store.* Free.

Pick 'n Pay
Supermarkets Hypermarkets
Our people make the difference

Explain how the visual-verbal cohesion works in the following Toyota advertisements

FIGURE 4.18 Toyota advertisement: efficiency

FIGURE 4.19 Toyota advertisement: dependability

FIGURE 4.20 Toyota advertisement: longevity

> ### Research and design
> Do research on Toyotas and then design your own font/word combination for the brand.

Section 5: Critical visual literacy

This is the second of the three sections that works with the semiotic resources that you need to be a text analyst. It was written by Ana Ferreira and Denise Newfield, except for page 98, Little *p* Design and Redesign, which Janks wrote. The focus here is on reading visual signs critically.

Two meanings of critical

It is important to understand that there are two different meanings of critical.

1. Critical reasoning is used to interpret the *meaning* of the text, based on an analysis of the choices made by the text-maker.
2. In critical literacy or critical visual literacy, the word 'critical' signals an analysis of *power, identity and access*. The positions on offer in texts are examined in relation to their *effects in the world*—the interests that are served by the text.

Reading for meaning requires interpretation and analysis. One has to understand how the choices made by the text-maker produce meaning. One also has to think about what the text is saying in relation to one's own knowledge, beliefs and values. In the role of text participant, the reader's or viewer's interpretation is based on the meanings taken *from* the text and the meanings he or she brings *to* the text. The reader as a text analyst considers the social consequences of texts and tries to understand what is at stake. Texts are judged in terms of how their representations and positions affect relations of power both locally and globally.

The four roles of the viewer

The four roles of the reader apply equally to visual texts. One has to understand the sign system that provides text-makers with options from which to choose. So, for example, with regard to shots, the text-maker decides between an extreme close-up, a close-up, medium shot, long shot or extreme long shot. Viewers have to be able to identify the shots used in images and they have to be able to *decode* them. Without the ability to make sense of the visual signs chosen, they cannot *participate* as readers of images.

Likewise, their experience in the role of image *users* will affect their ability to read visual texts. In the case of *The Spear* (p. 40), it was important for viewers to understand that this was a symbolic work of art, not a photograph. A user who is familiar with pop art representations of political figures, and with practices linked to the reading of art, would not have assumed that this was a depiction of the president's actual genitals as is suggested by the comment of one of his wives. Text users understand different genres of image and the viewing practices associated with the different genres.

What *The Spear* incident makes clear is that images have social effects and can be harnessed for political purposes. In this case some commentators believe that the image was used politically to construct the president as a victim of racism in order to get him re-elected. The relationship between this image and questions of identity, diversity and power were considered in Section 2. This text is a good example of the possible big *P* consequences of visual representation and the importance of the role of image *analyst*.

Visual signs

Many of the activities in Section 3 work with texts, which like *The Spear* are overtly political or confront social issues. Others work with more everyday visual texts. The main purpose of this section, however, is to give you practice in decoding, interpreting and interrogating the use of different visual signs. Visual concepts, the options for realizing them, and their positioning effects have been summarized by Denise Newfield and Ana Ferreira at the end of the section (pp. 99–100).

Point of view

Section 5 begins by explaining how a point of view is created in a visual image and invites viewers to consider three sets of questions to ask when looking at an image. These pertain to the content of the image, the way the content is portrayed, and the context of the image.

It might be useful to apply these questions to images that you bring to class. You can also apply these questions to images that you have encountered in earlier sections. What matters is that you look carefully and pay attention to detail. Page 86 focuses on looking at who is in the picture and why. Page 87 provides an image of a place and asks you to consider how the words construct a point of view for the reader and *anchor* the image, fixing it as a place of crime.

Visual genres

The theme of crime and the use of words to anchor a picture are continued in the next three pages, which provide questions to guide your analysis of a *photograph*. The issue of visual stereotyping helps us understand the relationship between images, positioning and power. Five pages on *political cartoons* follow.

It is the formal features of a text that enable us to recognize it as a genre—an instance of a particular type of communicative event—and the features of a political cartoon are explained on page 91. It is important to remember that genres guide our responses. When we know something is a cartoon we adopt a cartoon-reading position as opposed to the position we take up when we know something is, by way of contrast, a *portrait*.

Pages 92 and 93 compare a cartoon with a *painting*, and the cartoons about state presidents rely on our knowledge of *comic book* superheroes. Having looked at satirical representations of state presidents, the section moves to activities on Mandela and his construction as a global icon in a range of visual genres.

Little *p* critical visual literacy

The activities conclude with a reminder that the visual is also a part of everyday texts by inviting you to consider more ordinary genres such as book covers, packaging, web-sites and the visual layout of screens and pages. These are just a few examples of the everyday use of visual images. More can be found in Section 7 on everyday texts.

Multimodality

Many of the texts in this section are composed of both verbal and visual signs, and it is important to understand how these different sign systems work in combination. Multimodality is increasingly the norm for a wide range of texts that we encounter in daily life. Perhaps this is because new technologies have made it so easy to incorporate images into the texts that we produce. Or, it might be that we now need information delivered to us in segmented chunks, which require less sustained concentration than uninterrupted written text. You might like to consider other reasons for the wide use of visual images and to conduct some research on the range of visuals that you encounter over the course of a single day. Finally, it is important to remember that in a book it is not really possible to work with moving images, such as those we encounter in film, television and videos.

Power, diversity, access, design and redesign

As in Section 6 on the verbal and grammatical resources for critical literacy, this section focuses on the visual resources for design. While design and redesign are the central focus, how they affect power and constructions of identity and how they are affected by opportunities for access are what makes them resources for *critical* visual analysis.

CRITICAL VISUAL LITERACY

All images are constructed. Image makers make decisions about how to put their images together. Even photographs, which seem to portray reality, are representations.

Photographers decide where to point their cameras, how far away to stand from their subjects, what angle to create, whether to place their subject in the centre of the frame or off-centre, and so on. Cartoonists and other visual artists make similar choices about how to design their images.

Each person in the class should take one picture of the school—just one. Use a camera, your cell phone or sketch it in rough. If you sketch it, make sure you show exactly where the edges of your photograph would be and what or who would be included in the picture. Bring your images to class and compare them.

What decisions did you make—consciously and unconsciously—as an image maker?

What effect do these decisions have on how the school is represented?

Do different images make people think different things about the school?

FIGURE 5.1 Moral: where you point the camera changes what is represented

Re-read the elephant story on page 16. If instead of six blind men there were six photographers, and each photographer took a photo of only the section of the elephant s/he was standing next to, what would you see? What wouldn't you see?

Three steps in thinking about looking

WHAT/WHO?

The visual content:

Who or what is in the image? What do you see? What don't you see? Who is shown? Who isn't shown?

HOW?

Representation:

How are people, places or things represented? Shots? Angles? Lighting? Colour? Eye contact? Etc.

WHERE?

Context:

How is the image used? In what context—textual, social, political? What is the text's purpose/genre?

The *image maker* and the *image user* are not necessarily the same person. Newspaper editors and advertisers, for example, make choices about how to use the photographs they get from photographers. *The choices made by* image makers and image users position *viewers* to respond in particular ways. As critical viewers, we need to examine these choices and consider the *effects* they have on us as viewers. Most importantly, we need to think about *the social and political consequences* of these effects.

WHO'S IN THE PICTURE?

FIGURE 5.2

What kinds of people are selected for display on magazine covers? What kinds of people are not selected? Think about the 'ordinary' people we are used to seeing on popular magazine covers (i.e. not celebrities or other well-known public figures). How 'ordinary' are these people really?

> The choices magazines make about what kinds of women, men or young people to display on their covers say a lot about the kinds of people that society values.

'Ordinary' people on magazine covers seldom reflect the full range of people we find in the world around us—especially if you consider people of all genders, religions, classes, age, race, shape and size.

FIGURE 5.3

RESEARCH PROJECT

Visit your local magazine stockists and record the type of people you find on the covers of the magazines produced in your country. What conclusions can you draw?

Based on the women who are selected for the cover, what do you think counts as 'beauty'? What kind of women do you never, or hardly ever, see? Why not? Does it matter?

Googling interesting campaigns

Dove and the Body Shop, well-known brands in the beauty and health business, run innovative marketing campaigns that challenge narrow ideas about beauty. Dove creates adverts that include men and women who do not conform to stereotypical notions of beauty. And the Body Shop has created a doll called Ruby, the Anti-Barbie, shown in Figure 5.4.

Google the Dove campaign for real beauty and the Body Shop Ruby campaign.

FIGURE 5.4 Ruby

1. According to the official websites, what are the aims of these campaigns?
2. Have a careful look at the images used in these campaigns.
3. What kinds of women have been selected?
   - How do they differ from those usually found in conventional adverts?
   - What can you say about how they are being represented? Think about what kinds of shots and angles have been used. Think about their body language, gaze and facial expressions. How do these techniques help to convey a particular message about women and beauty?
   - Finally, ask yourself whether campaigns such as these are irrelevant or whether they can make a difference.

WORDS ANCHOR PICTURES

What do you see in the photograph below? How would you describe it? If you had to provide a caption for it, what would you say?

FIGURE 5.5

> The photograph was used in an advert for *Matrix*, a tracking system that can be fitted into a car to assist recovery if it is stolen. The words below are part of the advert. Read the text and answer the questions.

Anchorage

Photographs that do not have any text to guide the reader's interpretation can mean almost anything. Roland Barthes, a famous French scholar, used the term *anchorage* to refer to the way the surrounding words fix or 'anchor' the meaning of a picture.

With NoGo Zones from Matrix. If you're not supposed to be there, we'll know about it.

For a second, imagine that you are hijacked and kidnapped with your car. Imagine that you are tied up and have no way of reaching a panic button. Frightening isn't it? Now imagine that you are with Matrix. With our flagship MX3, Matrix introduces NoGo Zones, pre-programmed areas that we have identified as dangerous or unlikely for you to go to. When your car is taken into one of these areas, the Matrix unit sends a signal to our National Control Centre and we immediately send out the cavalry—without you having to lift a finger! Because Matrix's MX3 is constantly comparing the location of your vehicle against its database of known NoGo Zones, this is the ideal safety system for you and your family. So call 0800 77 99 88 and allow us to sell you peace of mind.

IT'S YOUR LIFE. IT'S YOUR CHOICE. CALL MATRIX 0800 77 99 88 FOR NOGO ZONES. WWW.MATRIX.CO.ZA

FIGURE 5.6 The verbal text that goes with the image in Figure 5.5

1. How is the verbal text (Figure 5.6) *positioning* you to interpret the photograph (Figure 5.5) in a particular way?

2. If your home was one of the ones shown in the photograph, would you be more likely to be an *ideal reader* or a *resistant reader* of this text? Explain.

3. Look carefully at the photograph itself. Does it match the idea of a 'NoGo Zone'? Can you notice details of the photograph that help you to '*read against*' the verbal text?

4. Design your own advert, for a product or service of your choice, using the same photograph in a completely different way. Explain how your text positions the reader differently from the Matrix advert.

PHOTOGRAPHIC CHOICES

Are the photographs below the same or different?

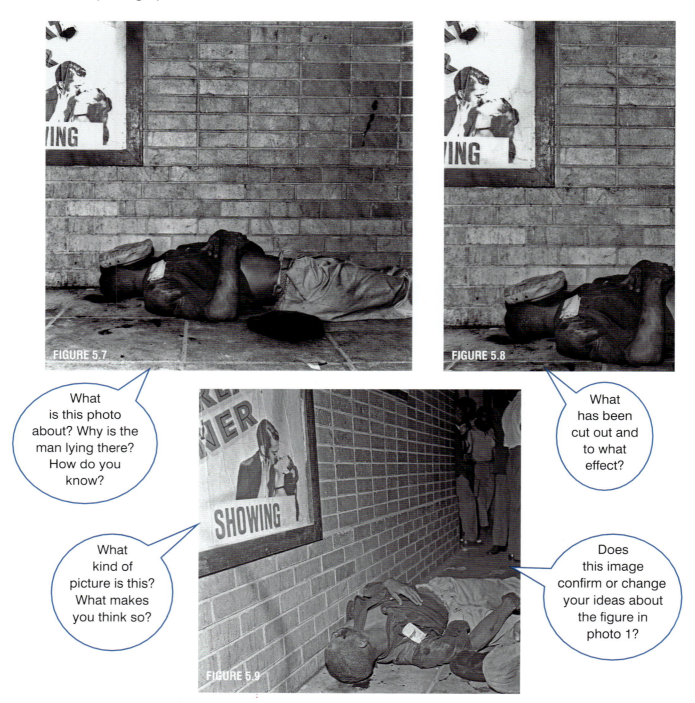

- How do the camera angles in Figure 5.7 and Figure 5.9 position you differently in relation to the figure of the man?
- How does the picture on the wall affect your interpretation of the photo? Think about the contrasts between the figures in the picture and the man on the ground.
- If you were a newspaper editor, which photo would you use for a front-page article and why?

ANCHORING THE PHOTOGRAPH

The photographs on page 88 were taken by Peter Magubane, a world-famous photographer. One of them was published in 1956 in the historic South African magazine, *Drum*, with a caption and article. Read the article to see how it anchored the photograph and positioned the reader.

FIGURE 5.10 Picture, *Drum* magazine

The caption reads: 'The Great Sinner' said Alexandra Cinema ad. Beneath, shot dead, lay gangster Mangena.

DEATH IN THE DARK CITY

Alexandra, April 1956

The whole Reef wants to know who killed Boy Mangena, thug, knifeman, bully and now just an unbefriended corpse. Boy was shot outside a theatre in Alexandra Township, Johannesburg, just the other day. Some people say a gang did it, others deny it, and others even say Boy was a gangster himself.

At any rate, Alexandra is in the grip of a serious crime wave. Everybody is living in terror as assaults, robberies and rape march on unhalted. The Dark City (Alexandra) is making Sodom and Gomorrah of old look like picnic spots for a Sunday School.

At the moment, a gang of the slickest criminals this city has seen, rules. There are other smaller gangs some of which are bracing themselves for a showdown with the big gang. But it would be a shame if police work should be done by criminals.

The people of Alexandra are appealing for protection, and not 'protection' of the kind that gangsters would like to offer them. It's about time that some tough policemen clean up the mess. It's not likely that the police know what's going on. Otherwise encouraged by their easy escapes the gangsters will become bolder and more dangerous. They should not be allowed to continue poking their tongues out at the law. Decent citizens have already given up going out to evening entertainment in this dark city of sudden death. They say it is not pleasant to hear the close whistle of a bullet near your ear in the dark.

It seems that Boy himself was one of those who traded in sudden death.

And the cinema outside of which Boy's body lay stiffening, was showing a film called The Great Sinner.

FIGURE 5.11 Article, *Drum* magazine

Discuss these questions

1. Alexandra is a township in Johannesburg. Why was it called 'the dark city'? What is a township, and how does it differ from a city? Do some research to find out.
2. What reason does the writer give for the crime wave, and what solution does the writer hope for?
3. Why do you think the editor chose the photo above rather than the other two photographs?
4. How does the caption fix the identity of the man on the ground? How does it link him to the title of the advertised film?
5. Does this photo stereotype townships? If so, in what way?

CHALLENGING VISUAL STEREOTYPES

Photographs present only the visual surface of a portion of reality. Visual stereotypes occur when a particular representation is repeated often and assumed to be the 'whole truth' without a full understanding of the context. Such stereotypes naturalize things that should be questioned or changed. If we set the photographs of Boy Mangena within the South African social and political context of the 1950s, it helps us to interpret it with greater understanding.

The extracts below provide glimpses of township life in the 1950s and today. Each extract *re-anchors* the photo of Boy Mangena in a new way. How does each extract provide you with a new position from which to understand Boy Mangena, gangsterism and township life as a whole?

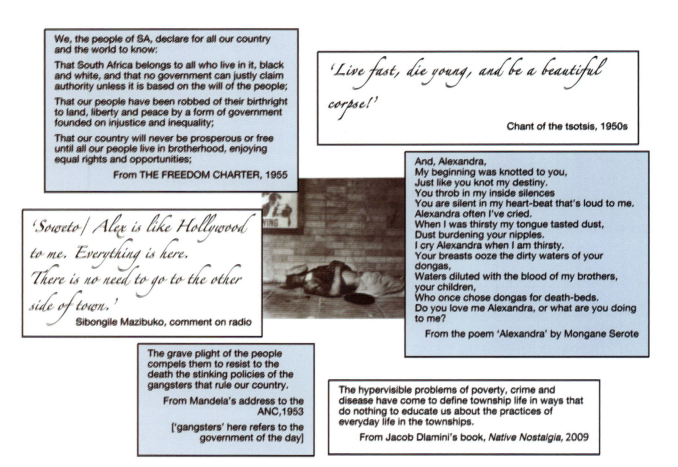

We, the people of SA, declare for all our country and the world to know:

That South Africa belongs to all who live in it, black and white, and that no government can justly claim authority unless it is based on the will of the people;

That our people have been robbed of their birthright to land, liberty and peace by a form of government founded on injustice and inequality;

That our country will never be prosperous or free until all our people live in brotherhood, enjoying equal rights and opportunities;

From THE FREEDOM CHARTER, 1955

'Live fast, die young, and be a beautiful corpse!'

Chant of the tsotsis, 1950s

'Soweto/ Alex is like Hollywood to me. Everything is here. There is no need to go to the other side of town.'

Sibongile Mazibuko, comment on radio

And, Alexandra,
My beginning was knotted to you,
Just like you knot my destiny.
You throb in my inside silences
You are silent in my heart-beat that's loud to me.
Alexandra often I've cried.
When I was thirsty my tongue tasted dust,
Dust burdening your nipples.
I cry Alexandra when I am thirsty.
Your breasts ooze the dirty waters of your dongas,
Waters diluted with the blood of my brothers,
your children,
Who once chose dongas for death-beds.
Do you love me Alexandra, or what are you doing to me?

From the poem 'Alexandra' by Mongane Serote

The grave plight of the people compels them to resist to the death the stinking policies of the gangsters that rule our country.

From Mandela's address to the ANC, 1953

['gangsters' here refers to the government of the day]

The hypervisible problems of poverty, crime and disease have come to define township life in ways that do nothing to educate us about the practices of everyday life in the townships.

From Jacob Dlamini's book, *Native Nostalgia*, 2009

FIGURE 5.12

Crime photographs today

Newspapers love to report on crime. Why do you think this is so? Look for images of crime in your local newspapers or on the internet, and cut or print them out. Bring your pictures to class and discuss them. What type of crime does it depict? What image has been used? How do the captions and articles anchor the images? Have the ways of representing crime changed since the 1950s?

POLITICAL CARTOONS

Like other cartoons, political cartoons are drawings that are humorous. But the political cartoon is a particular genre (type of text) that represents current events and political figures in a *satirical* way. By combining pictures and words, the cartoonist targets particular people and events and criticizes them by poking fun at them. A good political cartoon should not only make us laugh but also make us think.

When we examine political cartoons, we should consider the following key aspects.

Visual

The simplified and exaggerated style of drawing is called *caricature*. We recognise public figures by particular facial or bodily features that are exaggerated.

- *People*: Who is represented? How are they physically portrayed? What are the facial expressions and body language? How are they clothed? Are they holding anything?
- *Actions and interactions*: What is the person doing? If there is more than one person, how are they interacting? Where are they placed in relation to one another? What are their relative sizes?
- *Setting*: Where is the event taking place? When does it take place?

Verbal

Although political cartoons are largely visual, they also make use of words.

- Are speech bubbles or captions used to show someone speaking?
- What other words are present in the form of headings, banners or other bits of text?
- Is the style, shape or placement of the writing significant?

Words work to *anchor* the meaning of the cartoon. They can help us to identify people or events. They often provide commentary or shape our interpretation of events in a particular way.

Contexts

- *Media context*: Political cartoons are also known as editorial cartoons because traditionally they are found alongside the editorial column of a newspaper. The attitude or position of the cartoon usually reflects the newspaper's stance or *agenda*.
- *Social and political context*: The meaning of political cartoons is strongly linked to *when* and *where* they are produced and the *real-life events* of the moment. The more familiar we are with public figures and current events, the easier it is to understand a political cartoon.

As we have seen with other texts, political cartoons are positioned and positioning. The visual and verbal choices made by the cartoonists reveal their attitude or stance towards the subject matter—their position. These *choices* shape the way we interpret the cartoon, working to position us as *ideal readers* who share the cartoonist's attitude. But as critical readers we should be able to use our own beliefs and values to challenge the text. If we find the cartoon's assumptions problematic and we choose not to go along with them, we become *resistant readers*.

Have a look at the cartoon on the next page.
Read through the labels and answer the questions.

POLITICAL CARTOONS

SETTING

This is a scene from South African history, showing the first European colonizers arriving at the Cape. The Cape was already inhabited by the indigenous Khoi and we see two Khoi observing Jan Van Riebeeck and his men arriving.

1. What are the visual and verbal clues that enable you to recognise the *time* and *place*?
2. What are *your own attitudes* towards the subject matter—i.e. colonialism? How do you think these may *influence* your response to the cartoon?

PEOPLE

We recognise the different figures by their exaggerated characteristic features: Jan Van Riebeeck's long hair, moustache and pointy nose and chin; the Khois' pronounced cheekbones, broad noses and short hair. Notice the *contrast in the way the cartoonist represents the two different groups of people*.

3. Based only on the *clothing* and the different *objects* carried by the various people, which group would you say is *dominant*? Explain why you say so.

ACTIONS AND INTERACTIONS

The cartoonist uses *facial expressions* and *body language* to represent this interaction in a particular way. Van Riebeeck and his men stand confident and upright, and adopt stern facial expressions.

4. How can you tell whether or not the Khoi are intimidated by this show of confidence and power?
5. If we look closely at *composition* (placement of people within the frame), we notice that the standing Khoi occupies a higher position than all of the Europeans. What effect, if any, does this have on our interpretation of the situation?

FIGURE 5.13

6 April 1652

"WELL, THERE GOES THE NEIGHBOURHOOD!"

VERBAL TEXT

The words in quotation marks at the bottom of the frame anchor our interpretation of the event. At first glance, this cartoon seems to be a fairly conventional representation of a colonial interaction. It is the spoken words that overturn our expectations of the stereotypical colonial encounter and introduce the *satire*.

6. Are you familiar with this expression? What kind of people usually say it? About whom?
7. Here, who is saying these words? To whom? About whom?
8. Explain how these words reveal the cartoonist's own *position* on colonialism.

CONTEXT

This cartoon appeared in the *Mail & Guardian* newspaper, 4 April 2002. It is drawn by Zapiro, a South African political cartoonist who is well known for his hard-hitting, satirical humour. As a country, South Africa is an ex-colony and has recently emerged from Apartheid rule where white people owned most of the land. Issues of land ownership and redistribution remain unresolved and often surface in the media.

9. Is this cartoon only about the past?
10. Who would benefit from leaving land issues 'in the past'? Who wouldn't?
11. Do you think this text helps to maintain or to challenge current power relationships?

THE POSITIONS THE CARTOONIST CREATES FOR THE READER

What *effect* do you think the following have on you as a reader:

- the fact that we appear to be watching/viewing the scene from the perspective of someone who is standing on the land, slightly above Van Riebeeck and his men? (How would the effect have been different if we were watching the scene from the beach, for example?)
- the fact that, although the Khoi is obviously talking over his shoulder to his companion, his face is turned towards us?
- the fact that 'the neighbourhood' is really South Africa and that this cartoon appeared in a South African newspaper?

> The cartoonist has chosen to represent this event in such a way that the reader is positioned, like the Khoi, to view Van Riebeeck and his men as outsiders or 'Others'. In this way, he is criticising colonialism and positioning the reader to share his views.

Spot the difference

Sometimes a political cartoonist appropriates or 'borrows' an image that already exists in the public domain and alters it for the purpose of critiquing the original event or issue. Have a look at this painting. Compare it with the Zapiro cartoon on the opposite page.

A Scottish painter, Charles Bell (1813–1882) produced this painting to commemorate the arrival of the Dutch colonizers at the Cape in 1652. It is titled *The Landing of Van Riebeeck at the Cape of Good Hope*.

FIGURE 5.14

1. Do you think the similarity is a coincidence or has Zapiro deliberately created an alternative representation of the colonial encounter? What evidence can you provide for your answer?

2. It is the differences that carry the critique. Identify all the differences. Explain what it is about each of these changes that creates a new and critical meaning.

PRESIDENTS, SUPERHEROES AND INTERTEXTUALITY: OBAMA

FIGURE 5.15

Both of these cartoons depict political leaders as comic book superheroes. They rely on our knowledge of other texts—this is called *intertextuality*.

In November 2008, Barack Obama was elected president of the United States. The cartoon below was published in the *Star* newspaper in April 2009.

In April 2009, Jacob Zuma became president of South Africa. The cartoon on the next page was published later that month in the *Star* newspaper.

1. What do you know about Superman and the Hulk? How does this help you to make sense of these cartoons?

2. Does the way in which the superheroes have been matched to the political leaders influence your attitude? Would you respond differently to the cartoons if Obama had been depicted as the Hulk and Zuma as Superman? How does your own opinion of each of these political figures predispose you to adopting a positive or negative stance towards each one?

FIGURE 5.16

3. What physical features of each president does the cartoonist caricature?

4. Both leaders are presented as powerful. Does power have equally positive connotations in both cases? Provide evidence for your opinion.

5. How do the visual and verbal elements work together here to create religious overtones?

PRESENTS, SUPERHEROES AND INTERTEXTUALITY: ZUMA

Both cartoons are drawn by the South African cartoonist Wilson Mgobhozi.

The representational choices made by the cartoonist work to position us very differently towards each political leader/superhero.

What is your opinion of the students' comments?

The cartoons are drawn in such a way that one is a noble, respectable man and the other is a savage who abuses power—Thandeka.

The Superman cartoon directly opposes racial stereotypes by showing a non-white leader as so powerful, but in the same breath the Hulk cartoon reaffirms the stereotypical belief that African leaders are incompetent and brutish—Warren.

FIGURE 5.17

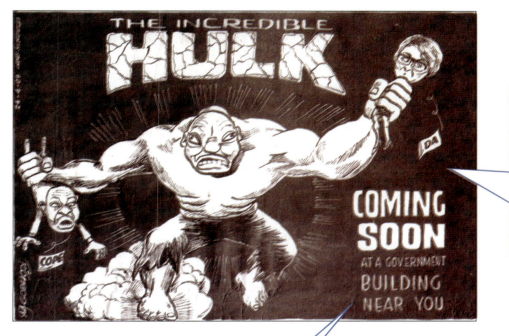

9. Who would be a resistant reader of this cartoon? What would a resistant reader say about what has been left out? Who would benefit from such a portrayal of President Zuma?

6. Compare the effects of the following visual features:

- facial expressions
- physique
- clothing
- background
- use of motion lines
- or anything else you find significant.

7. This sounds like the wording of a movie poster. How does this shape our attitude to this president?

8. Obama is standing on the spot while Zuma is running forwards. How does this create different viewing positions for the reader? Does it make us relate differently to the two men?

Collect different cartoons of the same public figure from different newspapers or cartoonists and compare the way in which the person is depicted.

Find your own examples of cartoons that rely strongly on intertextuality for their meaning. How does the choice of character or intertextual reference shape the way in which the public figure is represented?

REPRESENTING MANDELA: FROM INVISIBLE MAN TO GLOBAL ICON

Media images hold great power. They are seen by huge numbers of people across the globe. They inform us about events and people, shaping our view of things. They represent events and people from particular positions at particular times. Until the 1990s Nelson Mandela was represented as an enemy of the state and photos of him were banned in South Africa. Since then images of him began to appear regularly in newspapers, TV and film. Today books are written about him and international events are held in his honour. Once an enemy of the government, Mandela is now a global icon. Though no longer President of South Africa, his name and image are symbolic of political struggle, reconciliation and hope for humanity.

FIGURE 5.18

Examine the portrayals of Mandela on these two pages. Each picture represents a different aspect of Mandela's identity and history.

1. What identity of Mandela is constructed in each of the images? Consider the three steps of looking—*what, how* and *where*—discussed on page 85.
2. *When* is another important element of image construction. Each image captures a moment in Mandela's life. Number the pictures in chronological order. You may need to do some research into Mandela's life to complete this activity.
3. Using the central image as an example, provide a caption for each image. Choose at least two images that you will anchor in a negative way.
4. Do you agree with this selection of images or does it ignore the flaws of the icon? Using magazines, newspapers and the internet, select five additional images you feel could be included in this portrait gallery. They may be admiring or critical. Bring them to class and explain why you have chosen them.

DESIGN ACTIVITY

Choose a well-known local or international figure (sportsperson, pop star, politician, community leader or whoever) who is either loved or hated. Look through newspapers, magazines, books and the internet. Cut out, print or photocopy the representations of that figure that you find visually interesting or striking and that position viewers in particular ways.

Paste them onto a large sheet of paper or board as a collage or in another form. Your representation may be admiring or critical or a mixture of both. Provide a title that anchors your collage. Be prepared to explain to the class how your design reflects your attitude to the figure and attempts to position viewers in the same way.

FIGURE 5.19

FIGURE 5.20

FIGURE 5.21

FIGURE 5.22

THE INVISIBLE MAN
1962 -1999

FIGURE 5.23

FIGURE 5.24

FIGURE 5.25

SOON THE REVOLUTION
WILL BE OVER AND THEN
YOU CAN GO BACK
TO WORK

MASS
ACTION

BUST

BANKRUPT

INSOLVEN

LIQU

FIGURE 5.26

FIGURE 5.27

LITTLE P DESIGN AND REDESIGN

Google doodles

Google is the most widely used search engine. It resulted in the coining of a new verb—*to google*, meaning to look up information. To use Google one has to start on Google's home page, which receives over a billion hits per day. Since the beginning, Google has refused to sell advertising on this valuable page, preferring its clean, uncluttered look. However, since 2000, they have employed doodlers to play with the famous logo to celebrate holidays, anniversaries and people, creating over 1,500 redesigns. All the Google doodles can be found at www.google.com/doodles/finder/2012/All%20doodles. On this page you can examine the doodles by year (date tab) or by country (all doodles tab).

Examine the doodles for any year and see who was included. Who in your view might have been included but was not? What kinds of people get doodled? How many of these people do you recognize? Whose holidays are celebrated? Are the doodles appropriate for your country? What do you need to know in order to understand the doodles? Are the doodles serious, light-hearted, frivolous—what does your analysis tell you about the Google brand? What can you tell from the colours in the Google logo?

Apple packaging

Apple is another famous technology brand and its products, Apple computers, iPods, iPhones and iPads are highly desired consumer products. Steve Jobs, the CEO who turned Apple into the largest technology company in the world, did so by combining cutting-edge functional machines with beautiful design. Jobs understood that 'people do judge a book by its cover' and he therefore made sure that 'all the trappings and packaging of Apple products signalled that there was a beautiful gem inside'. His designer Ives agrees. 'I love the process of unpacking something. You design a ritual of unpacking to make the product feel special. Packaging can be theatre, it can create a story' (Issacson 2011, p. 347). Jobs understood how to create consumer desire.

Different groups should choose a category of goods that comes in packaging (for example food, candy, toys, equipment, tools, DVDs, computer games). Each group should collect examples of the packaging of different products within the category in order to compare and contrast the packaging. How does the packaging help to create a brand identity for the product? Discuss which brand different members of the group favour and why. Discuss whether it is important to have different brands to choose from or not. Does the world really need different brands of toothpaste? Cigarettes? Soap powder? Cars? Perfume?

Google and Apple website home pages

Compare the homepages of the Google (www.google.com/about/company) and Apple (www.apple.com) web-sites in order to examine how each company chooses to represent itself.

This activity required you to analyse the design of a screen. You should have noticed that you needed a new vocabulary that includes words like *navigation bar*, *tabs*, *drop down menus*, etc. What other words did you need?

Page layout

Now compare this page with other pages in this workbook and provide a critical visual analysis to support your comparison. Compare this page with pages like 27, 56 and 97. Redesign this page in order to make it more user friendly.

CRITICAL VISUAL LITERACY CONCEPTS: AN OVERVIEW

Table 5.1 outlines the key visual concepts used in this chapter. It focuses on the key *choices* made by an image maker and on the *effects* these choices have on how the viewer is *positioned*. To ensure that we are taking a critical approach, we always need to think about the *social and political consequences of this positioning*.

VISUAL CONCEPT	DEFINITION	EXAMPLES FROM CHAPTER	POSITIONING, i.e. effects and consequences
Type of shot	The distance of the camera from the subject determines whether we see the subject from close by or from afar. Range of possible shots: extreme close-up, close-up, medium shot, long shot, extreme long shot	1. An extreme long shot revealing many details of the informal settlement—shacks, streets, people chatting, children playing. 2. A medium shot of Mandela showing the bars of his cell. He is looking out and remembering his past as a prisoner	1. We look down on the scene from a distance. The anchorage of the verbal text positions us as middle-class observers of the living conditions of the poor, which we should fear and avoid. 2. The relative closeness brings us into a relationship of intimacy with Mandela, compelling us to engage with his mood. Because we are shown where he is we can understand his mood better
Angle of shot	The angle of the camera determines the perspective the viewer gets of the subject, e.g. high angle, low angle, eye level, aerial	In frame 2 of the Obama/Superman cartoon, Obama is drawn as if he is standing slightly above the viewer's eyeline, making it seem as if we are looking up at him	As viewers we are positioned to 'look up' to Obama not just literally but figuratively too. Despite the tongue-in-cheek tone, we are encouraged to view him as someone of importance and stature who inspires awe
Framing	The edges of the image act as a frame. The framing determines how much or how little of the surrounding reality is included in the image	In this photograph, Magubane includes not only the figure of Boy Mangena but also part of the urban setting—paving stones, the brick wall and a portion of the movie poster. The photograph tells a partial story	The frame limits the information we are given and brings objects into relation with one another. The juxtaposition of the corpse and glamorous poster invites us to consider issues of crime, urban living and disparities of class and race
Cropping	Cropping refers to the process of cutting off sections of the image. This shifts the edges and alters the initial framing	On the cover of Men's Health, the man's body has been cropped, emphasizing his toned torso. If this image were cropped at the shoulders as shown here, the faces would be the focus and we would not know what his body is like	Cropping is usually done when an image is used for a particular purpose, e.g. in a newspaper article or advert. By altering the image through cropping, the designers can deliberately influence our interpretation

VISUAL CONCEPT	DEFINITION	EXAMPLES FROM CHAPTER	POSITIONING, i.e. effects and consequences
Gaze	If the subject is looking directly at the viewer, the eye contact demands the viewer's attention. If there is no eye contact with the viewer, the subject is offering himself/herself to the viewer as an object of examination	1. Mandela is not making eye contact with the viewer. He is looking upwards, beyond the frame to the right, as if at a hopeful future that makes him smile. 2. Zuma has been drawn with diverging eyes and therefore, although he faces us, he is not looking at us	1. Mandela's lack of eye contact functions as an offer for us to observe him. We are positioned as admirers of this cultural icon and invited to share his optimistic attitude towards the future. 2. Zuma's unnatural gaze has a distancing effect. We are positioned to think of him as an animal-like being who is frightening and untrustworthy
Body position and body language	The way in which the subject's body is angled and positioned affects the viewer's relationship with the subject. A subject could be upright or lying down. The subject's body may be turned towards or away from the viewer. Gaze and other aspects of body language (e.g. stance, use of hands, etc.) also play a role	1. Ruby is shot from above. She lies in a bed of leaves, her body naked except for some leaves. One arm is raised seductively and her legs are crossed in false modesty. 2. Mandela is shown in a fighting stance, body turned slightly away from the viewer: wearing boxing gloves, fists raised to shoulder height and ready for combat	1. Ruby's body is daringly displayed in a way that we associate with thin, sexy women. We are deliberately invited to view Ruby as beautiful and sexually attractive, and to question stereotypical notions of beauty. 2. We are positioned as spectators of Mandela as a young boxer who is lean, powerful and ready for action. As viewers who know the older Mandela and all he has achieved politically, we are invited to look back and admire his fighting spirit
Composition and layout	The way everything is arranged in the frame creates a certain composition. This includes the way people and objects are placed, how they relate to one another, as well as the way the space is used	The cartoon is composed of four main elements: the sea with the ships; the landscape of Table Mountain; the group of colonizers with their flags, swords and guns; and the indigenous people	Because of their central placement and the dark coat and flag, our eye is first drawn to the group of colonizers and they appear dominant. However, the slightly elevated position of the indigenous people and their subversive comment undermines this dominance and positions us to side with them

Notice that although we need to think about each of these concepts one by one, they do not work in isolation. Positioning occurs through the combination of the various visual features as well as the written text.

Section 6: Time, space and bodies

This is the last section that focuses on semiotic resources needed for analyzing texts. It was written by Kerryn Dixon whose previous research has looked at how time and space are organized in schools and the effects that this organization has on young children's bodies.

In relation to printed texts, time is connected to sequencing. The text designer makes decisions about when the reader should receive information—what should come first, what should come last and how material should be arranged in between. An analysis of sequencing helps you to understand the assumptions writers have about their audience. Readers can of course subvert this order and decide to read in the order of what interests them most. Readers often skip pages or read the end of a novel to avoid the suspense. They can choose to skim or scan rather than read every word. This is a good example of how readers can assume agency in relation to how the writer is positioning them.

This book has been arranged into nine sections. You might consider the effects of this sequencing. Is it helpful or not? How does it position readers in terms of what they need to know, when? Do readers need knowledge from the earlier sections to complete the activities in later sections? Is Section 9 appropriate as the last section or should it have come first? What difference would it have made?

Time also affects the choice of material for a book. How soon do you think this book will be out of date? Will some sections remain relevant longer than others? Why?

In relation to printed texts the organization of space is most evident in layout and the amount of space given to different sections or activities. An analysis of the allocation of space in this book will give you a good idea of what the editor thinks is most important. Gunther Kress has argued that modern texts are modular with information organized into separate boxes. That is true of this book. It is worth thinking about how compartmental-ization positions readers. How does it affect the reading path—the order in which the page is read?

However, it is important to remember that not all texts in the world are printed texts. Classrooms are texts. Furniture is text. Gardens are texts. Cities are texts. Timetables are texts. Houses are texts. Objects are texts. Clothes are texts as are bodies. Toys are texts and so on, *ad infinitum*. How texts are chosen and placed helps us to understand positioning and spatiality. How people are organized into different parts of the city or in relation to geography affects their life chances. One of the things you notice in satellite photographs of the world is that there are no countries or borders. It is important to realize that these are man-made divisions that control people's rights of access and mobility.

Time is also a useful resource for analyzing non-print texts. Who decides for example when furniture is old and when it is antique? How are we positioned by diaries and deadlines? How are we taught to manage our time? Why does time have to be managed? How time and space is organized is different in different communities and this often leads to misunderstanding and conflict in contexts of diversity.

In this section Dixon starts by asking you to think about space, an abstract concept, in concrete ways. She invites you to think about the spaces you inhabit, the objects that are in them and the positive and negative associations you have with them. She then focuses on bedrooms and asks you to read them critically, bearing in mind that not all children have their own bedroom and some homes do not have any bedrooms. If you collect images of children's rooms from newspapers, the internet and magazines, you will learn a great deal about how such spaces are constructed in relation to wealth, gender and cultural norms.

Having looked at the home, she moves to the school. Here classrooms become the texts for analysis. It would also be worthwhile for you to consider how else space is organized in your educational institution. Which spaces are set aside for particular activities? What spaces are for staff only? Do any students have access to privileged spaces that other students do not have access to? How much room is there for your institution to grow? Are there some spaces that feel unsafe? Why? How cramped or spacious are the different areas? In what condition are the grounds and the buildings? How old is the institution? How does it celebrate its history?

Pages 103–105 focus on how people are expected to behave in these different spaces. What effects do these spaces have on our bodies—on how we are expected to sit, stand, walk, talk and so forth? Page 107 focuses specifically on how children's time is organized in and out of school. It is worth thinking about how much control you have over your own time and whether this is a good thing or not. At what age do you think people should be allowed and able to manage their own time?

The activities so far have focused on the everyday spaces of your lives at home and school or college, and could be considered as the small *p* politics of space. Now the work turns to the ways in which governments manage their populations and the effects of spatial planning and resource allocation.

One of the main features of Apartheid in South Africa was laws that regulated where different race groups could live, in which parts of the country and in which areas of the cities. This created impoverished rural areas and urban ghettos for people registered as 'non-white', whereas white people were able to live in well-resourced, leafy suburbs.

Another feature of Apartheid was strict control over people's mobility regulated by a system of pass laws. In South Africa, segregation was institutionalized by law, but in other countries there are more subtle means of spatial distribution. It is clear from these examples that geographies are connected to big *P* politics. Pages 108–109 ask you to think about your own contexts. Even spaces for the dead are not neutral and page 110 looks at cemeteries in different parts of the world.

The section ends with a consideration of mobility: who is allowed to go where and how this is controlled. Dixon extends earlier activities that asked you to consider constructions of refugees, migrants and foreigners. The last page of this section looks forward to Section 8 on digital technologies by introducing the notion of cyberspace and virtual realities, which enable our bodies to be both fixed and mobile at the same time.

It is clear from this section how space and time are linking to identity, power and access. Who you are, how wealthy or educated you are, together with how powerful or important you are affects your access to particular geographies, your ability to make choices and to design and control your environment.

BELONGING SPACES

Everything we do in our lives happens in space. Spaces like offices, schools and playgrounds have different functions. Space affects human relations (light, warm rooms can make people feel relaxed, while a dark, cold corridor can make us feel afraid). But human relations also affect how space is used. For example, spaces originally designed for one function can be transformed—in many cities warehouses have been converted into housing. Thinking about space and how space is used is a way of understanding how it is connected to our identities, our emotions, a sense of belonging and power relations.

It is important as human beings that there are places where we feel like we belong. In what space do you feel that you belong? Why did you choose this space? What objects are important to you in this space? (Where are they placed?) What sights, sounds, smells, or tastes make you feel like you belong in this space?

FIGURE 6.1 Spaces

FIGURE 6.2 Objects in space

FIGURE 6.3 Associations with spaces

> Which spaces make you feel like you don't belong? Choose one space and think about the objects and sensory experiences that make you feel like you do not belong. Compare your places of belonging and not-belonging with your class.

MY SPACE, YOUR SPACE, OUR SPACE?

For many people the home is where they feel they belong. The bedroom is often the room where we are most comfortable. It is where one can have private space. But having a room of your own is a luxury.

- Who gets to have their own room? Who makes these decisions? How are they made?
- Which groups of people have to share their sleeping spaces?
- Where do people sleep if they don't have a bedroom?
- What are the disadvantages of sharing space?
- What are the advantages of sharing space?

Read these two extracts from a web-site about designing bedrooms.
The arrangement of space and objects in space can tell us a lot about values and power

1. How are children and teenagers constructed in these texts?

2. If you were asked what makes a bedroom a belonging space for you how would you design a room for yourself? How does your design compare with these texts?

Kids adore fairy-tales, different stories about pirates and cowboys and surely cartoons. They often imagine themselves heroes of them. Girls play dolls and dream to be a princess or famous ballerina, boys collect comics about super-heroes and want to be as cool as them. You could make your child very happy by creating a bedroom which takes ideas from his or her favorite character (www.digsdigs.com/27-cool-kids-bedroom-theme-ideas/#ixzz1zTaF5Tyv).

Teenage bedrooms must have a very thoughtful layout. That's so because teenagers have a lot requirements [sic] that should be considered in their room. If you're going to design a room for your kid or kids by yourself you must do that. . . . You should consider: a lot of storage space, a thoughtful study place, a comfortable sleeping bed and a stylish look of the room (www.digsdigs.com/50-thoughtful-teenage-bedroom-layouts/).

3. Who is this text written for? What assumptions is the writer making about children and space for children?

4. Do you think these are the most important requirements for a teenage bedroom?

A photographer, James Mollison, became interested in the spaces in which children around the world sleep. As a way of engaging with children's rights he says, 'I found myself thinking about my bedroom: how significant it was during my childhood, and how it reflected what I had and who I was. It occurred to me that a way to address some of the complex situations and social issues affecting children would be to look at the bedrooms of children in all kinds of different circumstances.' You can find his photographs by googling 'James Mollison where children sleep'. Compare these spaces with your design, the texts above, and the photograph in Figure 6.4 of the bedroom of a girl who lives in a poor white Afrikaner squatter camp in South Africa.

FIGURE 6.4

A PLACE TO LEARN: CLASSROOM SPACES

relations. Analyzing the layout and organization of spaces can tell us about what is valued in terms of *size* (Who gets a big office? Who shares?), *location* (Who gets a good view? Who does not? Where is this space located in terms of other important spaces?), *the environment* (Is the space comfortable to be in? What kind of lighting, heat and ventilation are there?), *objects/resources* (Are there enough? Do they work?), *fixedness* (What is fixed and what can be moved or rearranged?).

Look at these three spatial maps from two schools in South Africa.

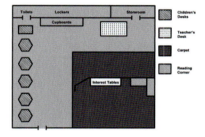

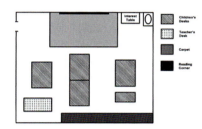

FIGURE 6.5
Spatial map of a Grade 00 classroom (4–5-year-olds)

FIGURE 6.6
Spatial map of a Grade 0 classroom (5–6-year-olds)

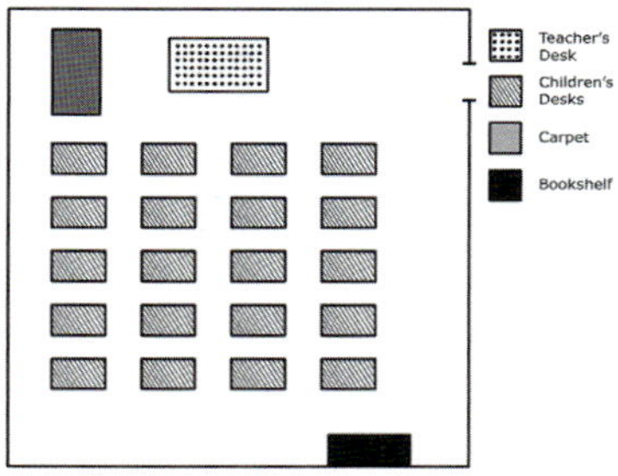

FIGURE 6.7
Spatial map of a Grade 1 classroom (6–7-year-olds)

Study these maps, answer the questions and then do the mapping project with a partner.

- What kind of teaching can be done and where?
- What kind of learning can be done (individual, collaborative, group)?
- What spaces can be used by the children?

- What are the power relations in these classrooms?
- What can you say about what it means to learn as the classroom organization changes over time?

Choose 3 or 4 classrooms that you think have interesting layouts.
Draw spatial maps of the classrooms.

Analyze these maps and compare location, size, environment, objects/resources, fixedness. What does this tell you about these classroom spaces?

What are the advantages and disadvantages of these classroom layouts?

Then analyze how these spaces are used (Who sits where? Is there space to move? Can you move through this space? Are you allowed to move? Who has access to the resource?).

What does this tell you about different ways learning and teaching are envisioned? Which do you prefer?

Based on your analysis how do you think classrooms should be designed?

TIME, SPACE AND BODIES

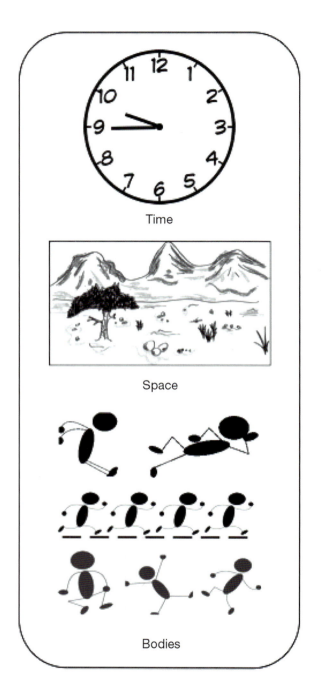

Time

Space

Bodies

FIGURE 6.8

What we do in space also happens in time, over time and across time. This also means that our bodies are trained to 'behave' in different spaces and times.

1. What time to you have to be at school? How much time do you spend at school?

2. Analyze your school timetable—what patterns emerge over a week?

3. How many school spaces do you spend time in on an average day? Where do you spend the most time? Where do you spend the least time?

4. Draw a mobile map of a typical day at school by drawing a map of your school and your movements through the school in a day.

5. For each new space draw a picture that demonstrates what your body does in those spaces. Look at the drawings of others in your class. Does a pattern emerge? What does this tell you about the schooled body?

6. Think about how the school manages bodies: are there spaces that have restricted access or that you are not allowed to access?

7. Are there rules for behaving in any classes?

8. Does your school stream children into classes, does it mark bodies with badges for achievement, does it have rules about what to wear and what you can look like?

9. How are you punished if you don't follow these rules? How do these punishments use space? What do they do to bodies?

FREE TIME

This is a weekly timetable for Cindi Berg. She is three years old. What do you think about how she spends her time? What questions does this schedule make you want to ask her and her mother?

	Monday	Tuesday	Wednesday	Thursday	Friday	Saturday
9-10						
10-11			Preschool			Soccer
11-12						
12-1						
1-2		Pottery Class			Dance Class	
2-3			Gymnastics			

FIGURE 6.9

Are you overscheduled? How much free time do you have? What do you do with it?

- I realize Cindi is an active child. She needs to keep busy.
- Experts tell us that children who have busy schedules thrive emotionally.
- It is important for her to learn skills and make friends. She will be exposed to activities and can decide what she likes later on.
- These activities don't develop creativity and imagination.

- Over the last 20 years children's free time has decreased by twelve hours a week.
- Some studies show that children who do too much are depressed, anxious and don't sleep properly.
- Too many scheduled activities affect family time and children often don't have time to do homework.
- She wants to keep up with her siblings!

How much time young people spend doing 'structured' activities is contentious. The term used to describe this phenomenon is 'overscheduled children'.
Read the comments from Cindi's mother and other people.
Do you think Cindi is an overscheduled child?

What is free about free time?

Parents and teachers are often concerned about how time is spent. Look at the following terms that are used to describe time not spent at school or doing academic work. How do these terms work to position adults and children?

Free time, spare time, recreational time, leisure time, structured play, unstructured play, backseat children (children who are taken to activities organized by adults), overscheduled children.

RESEARCH PROJECT
Interview friends and parents. How do they define free time?
How do they think it should be used?

MANAGING PEOPLE

Just as parents and schools can make decisions about how time is best spent and where it should be spent, governments also make those decisions for all of us. Governments are supposed to manage the population in ways that benefit everyone like having access to basic resources. They also need to know how many people live in an area or country, where they live, what they earn, to allocate resources equitably. Information about spatial distribution can tell us a lot about a place and the people.

> Can anyone live anywhere they want to? Are there any places you know where people can choose exactly where they can live? What factors affect the choices people can make about where they can live?

Look at the two maps produced by Bill Rankin of the American city Chicago based on the 2010 Census. www.radicalcartography.net/index.html?chicagodots

1. Who is represented on map 1 (Figure 6.10) and who is not?
2. What is interesting about the distribution of people in map 1 (Figure 6.10)? What does it tell you about the city of Chicago?
3. What do you think some of the reasons might be for this distribution? Write down a list of these reasons. Which reasons are connected to space (for example access to resources, infrastructure, the space itself)? What reasons have you listed but there is not enough information on this map to prove you are correct? What other kind of information do you require? Find this information to see if you are correct.
4. Which areas have high population density and which don't?
5. How does population density correlate with income in map 2 (Figure 6.11)?
6. How does population distribution correlate with income in map 2 (Figure 6.11)?

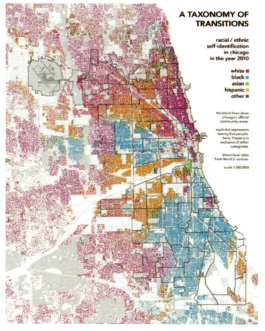

FIGURE 6.10

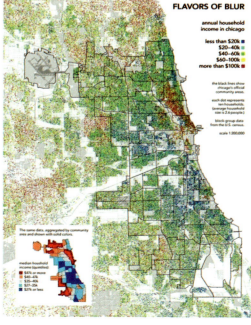

FIGURE 6.11

MANAGING PEOPLE: WHY ARE YOU HERE?

Not all governments have managed their populations in a way that benefits everyone living there. Sometimes they make choices that benefit one group over another, or they try to find ways to make people move out, and in extreme cases to try to make them 'disappear'. Here are two examples of immoral management by governments.

1. In South Africa the racist policies of the Apartheid government were reflected in the policy of 'separate development'. They created a mass of legislation to control where people could live, which areas they could work in, where they could go to school, and even which beaches, toilets and park benches they could use. Black people in white areas had to show their passes so they could legally be in certain areas. The government also forcibly removed people from their homes.

2. In Australia from 1869–1969 many Aboriginal children especially those who were mixed race or had light skins were removed from their families. Some argue that the policy was to look after neglected children but the Chief Protector of Aborigines in Western Australia A. O. Neville wrote in 1930, 'Eliminate the full-blood and permit the white admixture to half-castes and eventually the race will become white.' Some children were placed in orphanages, foster care or adopted by white families. Many never saw their families again. These children are known as the 'stolen children'.

Fiona's Story: 1936 it was. I would have been five. . . . We had been playing together, just a happy community and the air was filled with screams because the police came. We three, Essie, Brenda and me together with our three cousins . . . the six of us were put on the old truck and taken to Oodnadatta . . . we went to the United Aborigines Mission. . . . From there we had to learn to eat new food, have our heads shaved. . . . Then we had to learn to sleep in a house. We'd only ever slept in our wilchas and always had the stars there and the embers of the fire and the closeness of the family. And all of a sudden we had high beds and that was very frightening. You just thought you were going to fall out and be separated. There was a corridor and our cousins were in another room. We'd never been separated before.
(Bird 1998, p. 95)

Answer these questions:

1. What constitutes a belonging space in Fiona's story?
2. How does the action of the police work to invade the space?
3. How do the actions of the police construct the Aboriginal community?
4. What kind of cultural values and ways of being are contained in these two spaces?
5. How are spaces like dormitories organized that work against creating a belonging space?
6. What does such a policy reveal about understandings of children and childhood?

What other cases do you know of where people have been forcibly removed: Where have they been taken? What were the 'official reasons' given? What were the real reasons and what happened to them, or is still happening to them?

Why do you live in the city/suburb/area/neighbourhood you do? Has your family always lived there? Where is home?

What is the history of your family's movement through space?

Why do you attend the school that you do?

MAPPING YOUR NEIGHBOURHOOD

Reproduce Bill Rankins's map on a small scale by considering who lives in your neighbourhood. Think about other useful categories like language or gender you could use.

SPACE FOR THE LIVING AND THE DEAD?

Cemeteries often used to be on the outskirts of a city or town. But with expanding populations and urban growth, as this picture of Paris shows, they can be the view from your apartment block.

Another problem is that cemeteries around the world are running out of space. What space is there for the dead?

FIGURE 6.12

Move over, brother: big cities are rapidly running out of burial space

In the south-west corner of Soweto, a district in Johannesburg, lies the cemetery of Avalon, a vast swathe of rough grass and granite headstones that stretches as far as the eye can see. . . . Avalon is almost full despite three extensions that took it to 360 hectares, and so are many other cemeteries, including 27 out of the 35 in Johannesburg. In cities including Durban and Cape Town authorities are advocating 'secondary burials', where the deceased are laid to rest above another family member, or even 'reduction burials', involving the disinterment of remains after no fewer than 30 years and reburial in a smaller casket to create space. So far this has not proved popular.

Cremation could provide a solution. . . . Yet only 8% of South Africans opt for cremation, compared with a third in America, half in China, three-quarters in Britain and 95% in Japan. To many South Africans, cremation is taboo, not least because of ancestor-worship and a propensity to commune with the dead. Many prefer a burial in the countryside where they were born. It is what the ailing 93-year-old Mr Mandela has chosen for himself (3 March 2012, www.economist.com/node/21548976).

1. Do cultural beliefs need to change with the times or are burial practices and cemeteries important markers of people's identities, practices and values?

2. When cities run out of space for their living populations should the dead be moved? Who should make these decisions?

3. If you are buried does that mean you are buried forever? Will your body be moved like the bodies in the Paris catacombs with bones piled on top of each other? Practical, disrespectful or good for tourism?

FIGURE 6.13
Catacombs, Paris

FIGURE 6.14 Recoleta Cemetery, Buenos Aires

OMNIA MORS AEQUAT

DEATH MAKES US ALL EQUAL IN ALL THINGS

Or does it?

MOVING THROUGH TIME AND SPACE

As human beings who operate in space and time our movement through space, across spaces, into space and through time is part of our daily lives. But our ability to move and the means by which we can move are affected by social, legal, economic, educational and political factors. Class, race, gender and age also affect how mobile we can be. People's ability to move is an issue of access but also of freedom in small personal ways as well as in complex ways that relate to human rights and social justice.

Mobility raises many critical questions.

- Who can move and who can't?
- How far can they go?
- Where can they go?
- Can they come back?
- How do they get to their destination?
- Is there a destination?

FIGURE 6.15

Who we are affects our mobility. Use the identities of the following pictures to answer the questions in each role. How do the answers change? Why do they change? What issues does this raise?

Tourist   Refugee

Child   Stateless person

Migrant   Global Traveller

Emigrant   Illegal Immigrant

Name: _____

Status: _____

1. Does your location affect where you can go? How?

   Y ☐   N ☐

2. What do you need to know in order to travel? Do you have this knowledge?

   Y ☐   N ☐

3. Do you need documentation?

   Y ☐   N ☐

   If Yes what documentation do you need? Do you have it? Can you get it?

4. How will you get to your destination?

5. What can you do at your destination?

6. What will happen to you when you reach your destination?

7. Where will you stay?

FIGURE 6.16

Section 6: Time, space and bodies

FIXED BUT MOBILE

- Technology enables us to be physically located in a place while being connected with people who are not in the same place.

- What do you do that makes you fixed and mobile at the same time?

- What kinds of spaces can you enter by just being located in one space?

- What resources—old and new—do you need for this?

- If you are in cyberspace where is the boundary between the real and the virtual? Does there need to be a boundary? How does this affect your identity?

- How much time do you spend outside of the real?

"For the first time in [human] history, [people are] desperate to escape the present. Our newsstands are jammed with escape literature, the very name of which is significant. Entire magazines are devoted to fantastic stories of escape—to other times, past and future, to other worlds and planets—escape to anywhere but here and now. Even our larger magazines, book publishers and Hollywood are beginning to meet the rising demand for this kind of escape. Yes, there is a craving in the world like a thirst, a terrible mass pressure that you can almost feel, of millions of minds struggling against the barriers of time. I am utterly convinced that this terrible mass pressure of millions of minds is already, slightly but definitely, affecting time itself. In the moments when this happens—when the almost universal longing to escape is greatest—my incidents occur. [We are] disturbing the clock of time, and I am afraid it will break. When it does, I leave to your imagination the last few hours of madness that will be left to us; all the countless moments that now make up our lives suddenly ripped apart and chaotically tangled in time."

FIGURE 6.17

Source: Finney 2009 *American Fantastic Tales: terror and the uncanny from the 1940s until now*, Library of America.

Is Finney right? Are we breaking the barriers of time and space? Is this going to be catastrophic?

Section 7: Everyday texts

Doing Critical Literacy has so far included several texts that Barbara Comber, Allan Luke and Jennifer O'Brien call 'everyday' texts. These texts are mundane in both senses of the word—both ordinary and of the world. In previous sections, we have already looked at maps, CD covers, cards, posters, advertisements, comics, cartoons, movies, magazine articles, photographs and so on. Why then does this section focus on everyday texts?

It is important to make everyday texts an object of enquiry in critical literacy precisely because they seem so unimportant. They are everywhere. They come and go. We throw them away— food-packaging, newspapers, magazines, junk mail. We barely notice them. Yet these are the texts that present our world to us. They tell us what food to eat, which politician to vote for, what to buy, who can be trusted, who is corrupt, what we need to wear, what we need to think, who we can or should be. They decide what is normal and what is deviant. Advertising supports consumerism; bad news sells newspapers, and clothing becomes a marker of identity.

Even if we think they have no impact on us, that we are too sophisticated to be taken in by the version of the world presented to us in soap operas and Hollywood movies, there is a great deal of evidence to suggest that their effects operate below the level of our consciousness. In addition, we may be focusing on one message—which breakfast cereal is good for dieters—while not noticing that the message reinforces society's gendered ideal for women's bodies. Parents might be focused on which cereal their children like, while the children might be more interested in the 'free' toys included in their preferred cereal. Images of families, used to sell insurance or holidays, may wittingly or unwittingly naturalize the two-parent nuclear family and in so doing render single-parent or same-sex parent families as abnormal.

It is important to remember that everyday texts are often carefully designed to produce specific effects. Advertising agencies are employed to maximize design potential. Newspaper editors choose headlines intended to entice readers, even if the headline undercuts the message of the journalist's report (see, for example, the newspaper article on page 79). The positioning of such texts can tell us a great deal about what our society values, assumes, privileges, excludes.

While many of these texts deal with small *p* politics, they are connected to large and powerful discourses of individualism, capitalism, gender, class, race and nation. That is, to Politics with a capital *P*. Both kinds of politics are implicated in relations of power and everyday texts help us to see the working of power in our daily lives. They remind us of the importance that Paulo Freire attached to reading the word and the world. They are an embodiment of the worldliness of texts and their location in time (see page 25) and space (see page 77—the text on HIV/AIDS is specific to Southern Africa; see also The Columbine massacre, p. 73).

Section 7 was written by three different people. Janks wrote the opening section on modern ways of selling products that take us beyond advertisements. These developments require us to look also at branding and merchandising. Examining redesigned adverts produced by critics suggests ways for you to be creative in finding your own examples of marketing texts to write back to. Ana Ferreira looks at a range of everyday objects as texts— clothing, street signs and AIDS education texts.

Elsewhere Ana has also done fascinating work on signs for men's and women's toilets that she found on the internet. This gives you an idea of how creative you can be in examining signage.

FIGURE 7.1

Source: http://vectorart.org/.

FIGURE 7.2

Source: www.freepik.com.

FIGURE 7.3

In this section, Ferreira focuses on street signs in apartheid South Africa, because they show very clearly that signs are not neutral. She could just as easily have

looked at signs reflecting post-apartheid renaming.

The world abounds with examples of signage and she invites you to examine signs in the place where you live. Notice the gendered nature of this 'Please make up my room' sign found in hotels.

FIGURE 7.4

Stella Granville wrote the final part of Section 7 on newspapers as everyday texts. Stella has always used newspapers in her teaching. Here she looks at different kinds of newspaper texts: headlines, cartoons, articles and photographs. SMS text messages are included as part of the more recent interactive culture associated with news. She could equally well have used Twitter.

This section serves an additional function. Coming as it does after Sections 3, 4, 5 and 6, which give you tools for analyzing texts, Section 7 is designed to give you practice using those tools.

I chose to focus on everyday texts because it is precisely in these texts that signs are used to maintain, reproduce or challenge the status quo. Because they are so rooted in the everyday world, they also provide us with an opportunity to imagine or to investigate their social effects.

Their rootedness also makes selection difficult. We have tried to find texts that will make sense outside of our particular time/space context and hope that they will inspire you to find similar texts closer to your own time and in the spaces that you inhabit.

EVERYDAY TEXTS

Everyday texts are ordinary texts that we see in our environment every day: billboards, cereal boxes and other kinds of food packaging, toy catalogues, advertisement billboards, newspaper articles, websites.

Texts create positions for readers to take up. They include ways of valuing and believing that affect the way we think about our world. Ways of speaking and writing, discourses, shape us and we are often not aware that this is happening. These ways of thinking just become part of our everyday common sense. They become the ideas that we take for granted, that we think are natural. This happens when we are least expecting it—How many of us really imagine that advertisements and fliers and cereal boxes help to make us who we are? How many of us stop to read them critically?

1. Can you think of any others?

2. Why do they matter?

Foucault is a philosopher who thinks that 'Discourse is the power to be seized' (1970).

3. Why might he believe this?

4. Do you agree with Foucault or not?

Here are two everyday texts to begin with. Your job is to work out which can of Coke men are more likely to buy. You have to give reasons for your answer. Do you know why Coca-Cola is called *Coca-Cola*?

FIGURE 7.5 Coke cans

It's often said that Santa's red and white robes were the creation of a Coca-Cola advertising campaign. Do research to find out if this is true.[10] Either way why is this belief good for Coca-Cola? Why or why not?

EVERYDAY TEXTS—ADVERTISEMENTS

Look at the following advertisements that come from three different advertising campaigns for Liqui-Fruit, a pure fruit juice, produced and sold in South Africa. Each row of advertisements is part of a set. These adverts appeared in the same year in order from left to right. Each set is targeted at a different kind of buyer. Who do you think would find each of these different advertising campaigns appealing? Which campaign would make you buy the product?

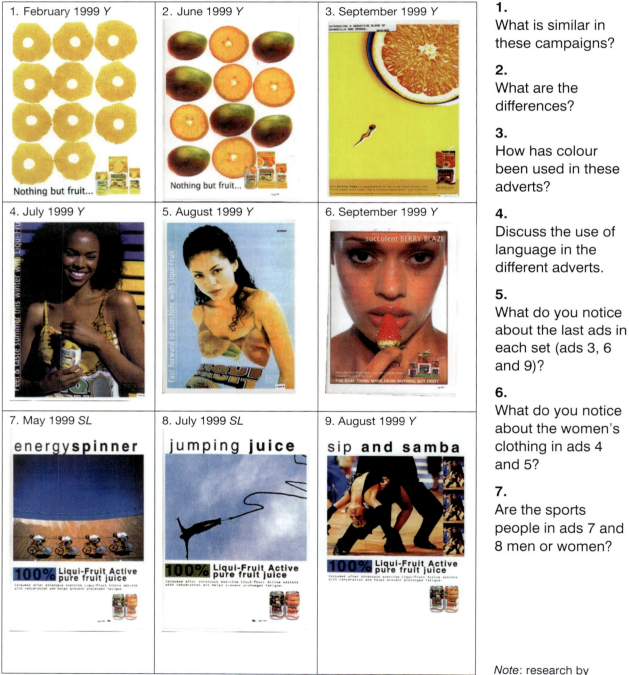

1.
What is similar in these campaigns?

2.
What are the differences?

3.
How has colour been used in these adverts?

4.
Discuss the use of language in the different adverts.

5.
What do you notice about the last ads in each set (ads 3, 6 and 9)?

6.
What do you notice about the women's clothing in ads 4 and 5?

7.
Are the sports people in ads 7 and 8 men or women?

Note: research by Sharon Weber, Wits University.

FIGURE 7.6 Liqui-Fruit advertisements

BEAUTY, SELF-IMAGE AND EVERYDAY TEXTS

Complete the following activities in groups. Once the groups have finished, Groups 1 and 3 should compare their collages; and so should groups Groups 2 and 4. The findings of these comparisons should be reported to the class for discussion.

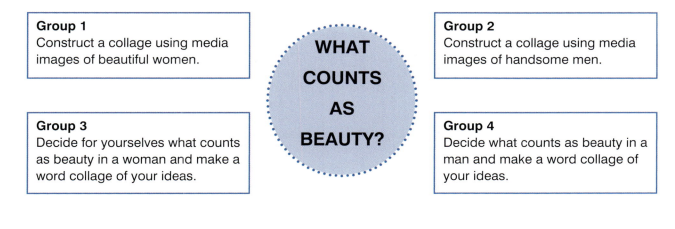

Group 1
Construct a collage using media images of beautiful women.

WHAT COUNTS AS BEAUTY?

Group 2
Construct a collage using media images of handsome men.

Group 3
Decide for yourselves what counts as beauty in a woman and make a word collage of your ideas.

Group 4
Decide what counts as beauty in a man and make a word collage of your ideas.

Good Hair—a documentary by Chris Rock

When Chris Rock's daughter, Lola, came up to him crying and asked, 'Daddy, how come I don't have good hair?' the bewildered comic committed himself to search the ends of the earth and the depths of black culture to find out who had put that question into his little girl's head! . . . the result is *Good Hair*, a wonderfully insightful and entertaining, yet remarkably serious, documentary about African American hair culture. . . . What he discovers is that black hair is a big business that doesn't always benefit the black community and little Lola's question might well be bigger than his ability to convince her that the stuff on top of her head is nowhere near as important as what is inside. (http://festival.sundance.org/2009/film_events/films/good_hair)

See the film if you can!

- Why do African American women use dangerous chemicals to straighten their hair?

Discuss.

- Does this connect with media images of beauty?

- What do black women outside of America think of black hair?

This young girl also thought she needed to change her hair. If you were her father what research could you do?

- How does this issue relate to questions of class, race and gender identities?

FIGURE 7.7 Hair

BRANDING AND BUY.OLOGY

Brands are more than just recognizable products associated with memorable logos and packaged with striking designs. What brands do is build an image around a particular brand version of a product. Martin Lindstrom (2008), a marketing guru, uses neuroscience research to explain how different centres of the brain light up when our 'buy button' is triggered.[11] He gives an example of how Coke used *American Idols* to improve its brand:

> During the show the three judges all keep cups of Coca-Cola in front of them and both the judges and the contestants sit on Coca-Cola curved chairs. Before and after their performances, contestants enter a room painted Coca-Cola red. Whether through direct advertisements or subtle imagery Coca-Cola is present 60 percent of the time on *American Idol*. Coke became part of the story of the show, with one of the judges even sipping Coke and telling another judge how much he likes Coca-Cola. By integrating their product into the show, Coke associated itself with the 'dreams, aspirations and starry-eyed fantasies of potential idols'. Want to be high-flying and adored? Coke can help. Want to have the world swooning at your feet? Drink a Coke. By merely sipping the drink onstage, the three judges forged a powerful association between the drink and the emotions provoked by the show.

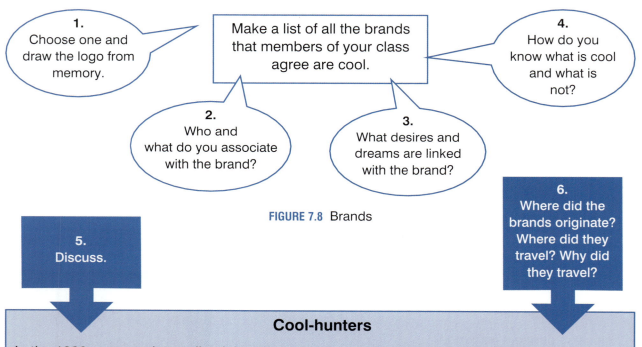

1. Choose one and draw the logo from memory.

Make a list of all the brands that members of your class agree are cool.

4. How do you know what is cool and what is not?

2. Who and what do you associate with the brand?

3. What desires and dreams are linked with the brand?

FIGURE 7.8 Brands

6. Where did the brands originate? Where did they travel? Why did they travel?

5. Discuss.

Cool-hunters

In the 1990s companies realized that teenagers were willing to pay to fit in and that peer pressure was a powerful market force. They needed to develop brand identities that would appeal to a youth market. So began the quest for 'cool'. The Superbrands, like Nike, began employing cool-hunters to follow teenagers around to find what was young and hip, at the cutting edge of youth culture. For example, the Hip-Hop style of young black men in inner cities was mined for cool. Ghetto cool was harnessed not just to sell it back to poor inner city youth but to a much larger market of middle class white and Asian kids all over the world, who mimic black style in everything from lingo to sports to music (Klein 1999, p. 72).

MERCHANDISING

Let's take Manchester United Football Club as a concrete example to explain what is meant by merchandising. First you watch soccer, then you support Manchester United, then you buy the kit: the scarf, the hat, the jersey, the boots, the mitts, then you buy the poster, then the football cards for your sticker book, then the bag and the towel and the toothbrush and the toys.

Merchandising is a way of selling goods in which you use the brand or image from one product (e.g. *Star Wars*) to sell another product (e.g. figures, clothing, toys, mugs). The owner of the brand (*Star Wars*) controls the merchandising and often makes much more money from this than from the original product.

FIGURE 7.9

Who is the main target market for merchandising?

What merchandise do you like? Why?

Give other examples of merchandising. Think of products for young children, for young adults and for adults.

Walt Disney was a genius at converting a movie into additional money (the Mickey Mouse watch and Dell's Disney comic books, not to mention the TV shows and theme parks). But when *Star Wars* became a cultural phenomenon, every kid had to have the action figures, light sabers, key chains, games, books, pajamas, etc. Lucas all but created the market for collectibles and, in the process, made himself a billionaire. Since 20th Century Fox let him keep the merchandising rights, he got to keep the money they made. He earned more from the spinoffs than from the movies.

(Adapted from www.time.com/time/specials/2007/article/0,28804,1625074_1625073_1625067,00.html)

FIGURE 7.10

FIGHTING BACK—DISCOVER CULTURE JAMMING AND ADBUSTERS

When companies have products to sell, they have to make us want to buy them. So they have to turn people into consumers and the sellers target younger and younger buyers. For example, children all over the world recognize McDonald's Golden Arches and the happy meal toys that go with them. We learn to be consumers from our seats in supermarket trollies.

'CAPITALISM DEPENDS ON CONSUMERISM'

Just after 9/11 Bush, famously, told the American public: 'Fly and enjoy America's great destination spots. Get down to Disney World in Florida. Take your families and enjoy life, the way we want it to be enjoyed.' He even asked consumers to spend during better times. 'I encourage you all to go shopping more,' he said in December 2006.

(http://blogs.wsj.com/economics/2008/10/07/)

Explain.

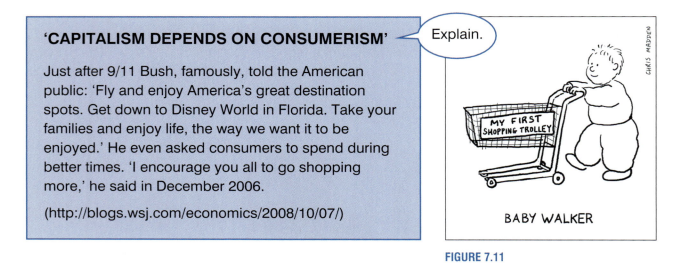

FIGURE 7.11

Research project

Adbusters are a network of 'culture jammers' and creatives all over the world who are 'working to change the way

- information flows
- corporations wield power
- meaning is produced in our society' (www.adbusters.org).

Produce your own spoof ads.

Find out what culture jammers are and how they attack advertising with campaigns and spoof ads.

FIGURE 7.12

FIGURE 7.13

CLOTHES AS EVERYDAY TEXTS

The clothes we wear are not just protective body covering; neither are they only about fashion. They are also an expression of identity, belonging and allegiance—of who we are, what we believe and who we aspire to be.

If we think of *clothes as everyday texts*, does it mean that the person wearing the clothes is '*the writer*' and the person looking at the clothes is '*the reader*'?

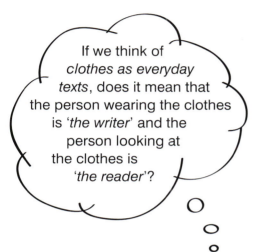

It's not only what you wear, it's how you wear it

Holden Caulfield is the protagonist of *Catcher in the Rye*, a classic American novel of teenage rebellion (J. D. Salinger, 1951). He has a red hunting cap that he usually wears with the peak around the back, symbolising his rebellion.

What type of headgear is common nowadays? Are there different ways in which it can be worn? Do these project a different identity for the wearer?

FIGURE 7.14

The two styles alongside come from an article on jeans from *SL* magazine (May 2006). This is the introductory paragraph:

> Usually you can tell what music someone's into by the jeans they're wearing. But these days there are so many options the signals can blur a little. So we've put together this handy little guide for decoding denim.

Do you agree that it is possible to 'decode' people's clothing to work out what type of person they are? When does it work? When does it not work?

Do you fit neatly into a definable style or do you borrow elements from various styles? Or is your style constantly shifting? Draw yourself in your favourite set of clothes and write a descriptive paragraph that explains what your clothes say—or do not say—about you.

FIGURE 7.15

COSTUMES

FIGURE 7.16

Costume designers create the look and identity of each character by designing their clothes and accessories. They have to do research into time and place in order to capture the period of the movie. They have to understand the script in order to create a fit between the characters and their costumes. Costumes position us to make judgements about characters.

The same is true of costumes in everyday life. Look at the pictures below, of the Queen of the United Kingdom, Winston Churchill, Nelson Mandela, Mahatma Gandhi. What costumes have they chosen for themselves? What cultural knowledge is needed to decode these pictures? How do their styles compare with those of modern-day leaders?

Now look at yourself and the people around you. What images do people create for themselves by the clothes they wear?

FIGURE 7.17

WEARING YOUR POLITICS ON YOUR SLEEVE

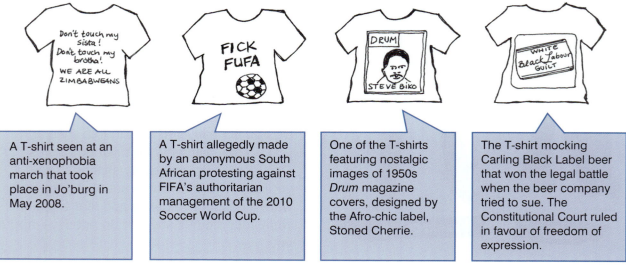

A T-shirt seen at an anti-xenophobia march that took place in Jo'burg in May 2008.

A T-shirt allegedly made by an anonymous South African protesting against FIFA's authoritarian management of the 2010 Soccer World Cup.

One of the T-shirts featuring nostalgic images of 1950s *Drum* magazine covers, designed by the Afro-chic label, Stoned Cherrie.

The T-shirt mocking Carling Black Label beer that won the legal battle when the beer company tried to sue. The Constitutional Court ruled in favour of freedom of expression.

FIGURE 7.18

EVERYDAY TEXTS ON HIV/AIDS

South Africa has one of the highest HIV/AIDS infection rates in the world. Because young people are particularly vulnerable to this disease, many AIDS awareness campaigns are aimed at youth. One way of trying to reach young people is through the informal everyday texts that they come across in their environments, such as billboards, youth magazines and even branded marketing.

Young Designers Emporium (YDE), a fashion outlet for the young and trendy, ran an AIDS awareness campaign called 'Fun with Dick and Jane'. At their stores they handed out booklets entitled 'Let's learn safe sex' containing reading cards (like the one alongside) and a free condom.

FIGURE 7.19

1. The images and wording are modelled on the classic schoolbooks used by young children to learn to read. How does this choice affect how you respond to the content?
2. Look closely at all aspects of the card. Is this text only about safe sex? What kind of young person does this text suggest you should be, or look or behave like?
3. Use the internet to find out which global youth brands do AIDS awareness work and what they do.

Revision

S___ sex means using a condom every time.

Finish the word

answer: safe

FIGURE 7.20

'Jane wears jeans by Milla, vest by Funk. Dick wears shirt by Billionaire, jeans: Dick's own'.

This is a magazine advert for Yfm, a popular music station for urban black youth.

How does this advert position you?

How do you think the Yfm brand might benefit from this ad?

FIGURE 7.21 'Safe sex is the best protector against AIDS. Use a condom or you'll end up between these sheets.'

In your opinion—What effects, if any, do texts like these have on their young readers? To what extent do they influence attitudes and behaviour towards HIV/AIDS?

Section 7: Everyday texts

STREET SIGNS: EXCLUSION AND OTHERING

Signs in public places are another type of everyday text. Like other texts, they do not simply provide us with neutral information—they often tell us how to behave, where to go and where we can and cannot be. In South Africa during the Apartheid years, signs were used to enforce racial segregation: by law black and white people lived in separate areas, used separate public transport, attended separate schools. Black people were treated as second-class citizens and the signage was evidence of this.

Race

FIGURE 7.22

FIGURE 7.23

This is the kind of sign you would have seen on the beaches, which were places of privilege reserved for white people. Such signs were commonplace and made social inequalities seem 'natural' and beyond question. Now it is hard to believe that such signs existed and to see them we would need to visit the Apartheid Museum. The photograph on the left shows the entrance to the museum, which has been built so that visitors experience the segregated conditions for themselves as they enter.

Apartheid signs may now be kept in museums but that doesn't mean that inequalities and exclusion are a thing of the past. Can you think of current signs that exclude people from certain places?

In the United States, the marketing campaign for the science fiction film *District 9* consisted of billboards and other public signs that were a deliberate imitation of Apartheid-style signage. These signs reflected the ways in which the aliens are treated by the citizens of Johannesburg. The film can be read as an allegory of Apartheid.

FIGURE 7.24

INVESTIGATING SIGNAGE

Do an image search on Google for 'whites only' signs. Choose three different signs that are not from South Africa. Try to place them in their historical context. In other words, where and when were they used?

What was going on in that society at the time? Who benefitted from this kind of social exclusion? What other kinds of exclusionary signs exist today? Are there signs that we are so used to seeing in our everyday lives that we no longer notice how they are working to exclude others?

This is a made-up sign. Can you think of a place where a sign like this would accurately reflect people's unspoken attitudes?

FIGURE 7.25

Section 7: Everyday texts

EMAIL—REDEMPTION THROUGH READING

People who have email accounts are constantly bombarded with texts, in many different genres. Like other everyday texts, we often read them and move on, without considering their social effects in relation to power, access or identity or paying attention to their design. The email below is in the exact form in which it was received, using the email function on a news feed. It offers an interesting perspective on literacy.

From: John Janks <John.Janks@belldewar.co.za>
Subject: Brazil reading move
Date: 28 June 2012 10:52:02 AM SAST
To: Hilary Janks <hilary.janks@gmail.com>

General: Brazilian prisoners can read to reduce their sentence Brazil will offer inmates in its crowded federal penitentiary system a new way to shorten their sentences: a reduction of four days for every book they read, says a *BBC News* report. Inmates in four federal prisons holding some of Brazil's most notorious criminals will be able to read up to 12 works of literature, philosophy, science or classics to trim a maximum 48 days off their sentence each year, the government announced. **Prisoners will have up to four weeks to read each book and write an essay that must 'make correct use of paragraphs, be free of corrections, use margins and legible joined-up writing',** said the notice published in the official gazette. A panel will decide which inmates are eligible to participate in the programme, dubbed Redemption through Reading. 'A person can leave prison more enlightened and with a enlarged vision of the world,' said São Paulo lawyer Andre Kehdi, who heads a book donation project for prisons. **Full BBC News report**

Regards
John Janks

- How does this text construct literacy? Why might the authorities in Brazil believe that *Redemption through Reading* is possible? What do you believe?

Why has the word redemption been used? Food for thought:

'The truth will set you free' (John 8.32).

- What kind of texts do they have to read? Why these texts and not others? What language do you think these books will be written in?

- What kind of language and handwriting are prisoners expected to write in order to earn the days off their sentence?

- How are the prisoners constructed?

- How do the constructions of literacy and the prisoners relate to questions of access, power and identity?

- 'Full BBC News report' is a hotlink to the BBC website, www. guardian.co.uk/world/2012/jun/ 26/prisoners-books-reduce-sentence.

FIGURE 7.26

Note: Jerry Harste's student's representation of literacy with a red book shown beyond the bars of the cell.

NEWSPAPER TEXTS

READ ALL ABOUT IT !!

NEWS

FIGURE 7.27

FIGURE 7.28 The slogan of a Johannesburg newspaper

'The Star tells it like it is'

Can you 'read all about it'? Why? Why not?

Can any newspaper 'tell it like it is'? Why? Why not?

Indicate *true* or *false* to the following statements.

- You can find out what's happening in the world if you read the newspapers.
- It is better to look on the internet to get the real news.
- Newspapers tell us the hard facts.

Sports headlines position teams.

- How is the South African team positioned in the headlines below by different newspapers?
- How is your favourite team positioned by the headlines in different newspapers?

WORLD CUP LIVES ON FOR SOUTH AFRICA

The Star

SOUTH AFRICANS AROUND THE COUNTRY CELEBRATE AS BAFANA BAFANA BEAT FRANCE 2–1 IN BLOEMFONTEIN YESTERDAY

HEROES!
They came to make South Africa proud and **they did.**

The Sowetan

WHAT A GRAND EXIT!
Bafana may be out of the World Cup, but their 2–1 win over France did us proud.

The Times

FIGURE 7.29

Bring the front page of two different newspapers published on the same day to class.

- Compare the *choices* for the front page made by the editors of the different newspapers. Explain the effects of the different choices.
- Find out who is the target readership for each of the newspapers. How does this affect the choices made?
- What gets into the news? What would you and/or the members of your group have put on the front page?

Choose a day. Design a front page for that day and compare your page with those of your classmates. Discuss the differences and try to account for them.

POSITIONS ON NEWS ISSUES

The secularity law in France, sometimes referred to as 'the veil law', was voted in by the French parliament in March 2004. It forbids the wearing of any 'ostensible' religious articles, including the Islamic veil, the Jewish kippa, and large Christian crosses. Read the following article. Look at the words and the image to decide on how the text has been positioned.

Ban thinly veiled Islamophobia
20 APR 2011 00:00

Can you imagine a law in South Africa prohibiting Muslim women from wearing the veil? Or banning Jewish men from wearing a yamulkah, or Sikh men from wearing a turban? Since April 11 this has been the situation in France. It has banned the wearing in public of face-concealing veils such as the niqab or burka. Offenders can be stopped by police and given a nominal, but symbolically powerful, fine.

This is a sad day, not only for freedom of religion but for equality. Why is this so? The law is rooted in the long-standing French policy of cultural integration and the pursuit of a uniform French identity (we can call this the pursuit of equality through equivalency—we're all treated the same because we all, somehow, are the same).

In truth, the ambition of cultural integration has been a project of cultural imposition, where the dominant French identity (white, European and Christian) has become the gold standard for all communities living in France. The riots that

FIGURE 7.30

have beset communities of African descent are, at the very least, a sign that this integration is not going well because it is about the thinly veiled (pun intended) imposition of French (read: European) culture, over foreign (read: African and Arabic) cultures.

This new legislation is also embedded in France's insistence that it is a secular society. The claim is disquieting, insincere and a deep insult to immigrant communities in France. Does France not celebrate Christmas, a public holiday? And Easter? Does it not put the famous churches, the Sacré Coeur and Notre Dame, at the forefront of its list of treasures, as emblematic of its national identity?

So this law is not about secularism or the separation of church and state, but about

cultural uniformity, the rejection of difference and, if we're honest, a deep discomfort with Islam.

Which brings us back to the veil. The French also claim that the law is a feminist initiative. Let me be clear: every community, including Muslim ones, has practices that discriminate against women and it is not only appropriate but a legal requirement under international law that states legislate to ensure that women enjoy equality with men. One of the key features of the women's movement is to ensure that women's health, wellbeing, potential and ambitions are not thwarted by the state, cultures, communities or families.

But banning the veil does not achieve this. Its consequence is that Muslim women in France who wear the veil, willingly or not, will not be allowed in public without incurring a fine. This is extremely dangerous for women and a blow for immigrant women's rights.

The author, Bonita Meyersfeld, is a professor of law at Wits University

FIGURE 7.31

Source: http://mg.co.za/print/2011-04-20-ban-thinly-veiled-islamophobia.

Research the issue of the veil ban on the internet, where you will find a range of articles written from a range of different positions. Then, rewrite this text taking a different position.

COMPARING THE NEWS

In March 2010, the South African President's visit to England 'hit the press'. In your opinion, why does an event of this nature make the headlines? Many different kinds of articles (cartoon, news article, editorial, readers' views) appeared in both the British and South African newspapers. Identify the different types of texts that appear on this and the next page and explain how they differ.

TRIP TO SEE THE QUEEN COSTS SOUTH AFRICA R8 MILLION

THURSDAY MARCH 4 2010   Established 1887
47 Sauer Street, Johannesburg

The filth of Fleet Street

THAT the British press used the occasion of Jacob Zuma's State visit to Britain to attack our polygamous president over the number of his wives and children, and his sex life, should have come as no surprise.

Neither should the viciousness of the attack from those sections of the UK press that either make their living in the gutter, or are of such a right-wing persuasion that they have been desperate to see South Africa fail ever since predicting a bloodbath would follow the advent of the country's democracy in 1994.

Zuma does lay himself open to being parodied, and the South African press has had a field day with him in the past and will no doubt do so again in the future, but the lengths to which some of the British tabloids sunk says more about them than it does about Zuma or South Africa.

These are the same newspapers which, in their desperation to show South Africa was not ready for or fit to stage the World Cup, last week used month-old pictures of England's under-construction training base in Rustenburg to "prove" 2010 was a disaster in the making.

But the excesses of the UK tabloids are a sideshow to Zuma's visit, with the substance coming from the large business delegation which has accompanied him. Britain remains one of South Africa's major trade partners, and the top source of tourists to the Republic. As for the hosts, they select the countries afforded state visits on the basis of their commercial and political importance to themselves. Zuma's most important task on this visit is to reassure investors that South Africa is not going to nationalise its mining industry, and that in an uncertain world the country remains the safest and one of the most attractive of the developing economies to invest in. Where Zuma is likely to differ with his hosts is on the issue of Zimbabwe, where he supports the lifting of targeted sanctions against the Zanu-PF elite, using the strange argument that they somehow justify being rewarded.

As for the bigots of the sex-obsessed UK tabloids, he can ignore them.

FIGURE 7.33

FIGURE 7.32

Zuma may be a polygamist but he doesn't lop off heads

WELL done The Star: your editorial ("The filth of Fleet Street", March 4) in which you side with President Jacob Zuma and hammer the British tabloids is admirable.

At home we criticise and attack him, that's true, but when he is abroad we say "hands off our president!"

I worked in London for five years and what Oscar Wilde wrote is certainly true for the tabloids: "An editor's conscience is there purely for decorative purposes."

They may mock his culture and say his polygamy and promiscuousness are contrary to religious beliefs but their own King Henry VIII, when confronted with marriage problems, simply broke away from the Roman Catholic Church and formed his own. When he had wife problems he imprisoned them or lopped off their heads.

And talk about ego: the monarch had one poor individual with the exalted title of "groom of the stool" who had the job of inspecting the "royal turds" in the morning so that a panel of physicians could ascertain the king's health and moods for the day.

Zuma is on a business trip. Allow him to concentrate on that because it is of benefit to both countries.

At home he has problems to face that will probably not make him happy when he sees the African continent come into view on his return journey.
Cliff Saunders
Northcliff, Joburg

FIGURE 7.34

SOUTH AFRICAN PRESIDENT MEETS THE QUEEN

FIGURE 7.35

SMSs

SEND YOUR VIEWS TO 32212

▪ *SONILE Nokuthula, so you agree with Zuma and his many wives, do you? How many wives has your husband got? No backward cultural practice for this black sister.*
LONGILE

▪ *SONILE Nokuthula, your opinion of March 4 is just a lame attempt to whitewash JZ's tarnished image and Mugabe's madness. Try again.*
MUNTU

▪ *SONILE Nokuthula, respect is earned, not deserved. This applies to Zuma as well.*
ROOSTER

28 *Mail&Guardian* March 5 to 11 2010
Comment&Analysis

Royals shock Zuma

FIGURES 7.36 & 7.37

Right royal protocols for Zuma's palace stay

Mandy Rossouw

I was clear from the start that Queen Elizabeth II, a stickler for rules, was going to be a good, if stern, host.

The Zuma party was settled into its own living quarters in the palace, which has, according to South African head of state protocol Kingsley Makhubela, more than 400 rooms. The president's corner of the palace also boasts its own entrance and a fully equipped office.

But what may sound like a teenager's dream came with a predictable spanner in the works — a curfew.

According to Makhubela, the Buck House flunkies made it plain that they expect all guests to be home and tucked up in bed — preferably their own — by midnight.

"They were very clear in reminding us that you can't come in late at night," he said. "This is not like a hotel, where you can come and go as you please and they asked us not to come in at 1am and disturb the queen."

A simple handshake was also a carefully considered matter. "You know how South Africans give you a handshake that shakes your whole body? For the queen it must be different; the handshake needs to be of a much softer touch."

Ever the gracious host, the queen threw a banquet for her new South African friends on Wednesday evening in the palace ballroom, but even that did not get under way without a few golden rules being learned off by heart.

Men have to remember to bow when they meet the queen, but unlike the Chinese, who bow from the waist down, the English prefer a brief but distinctive nod.

Women are not expected to curtsey, but they do have to wear long dresses: miniskirts are forbidden. Tailcoats and white ties are obligatory for men.

Not short on good manners himself, Zuma brought the queen a ceramic artwork from the popular Ardmore studio in the Champagne Valley in KwaZulu-Natal.

Prince Philip will be treated to a chess set with crafted Nguni warriors as pieces.

FIGURE 7.38

Questions to consider

1. How is the President represented by the
   * British media
   * South African readers in their letters and text messages
   * newspaper editorial
   * photographs?

2. How is the British press represented by the South African newspapers articles and cartoons?

3. How is the Queen constructed/represented by the
   * articles in the South African press
   * cartoons?

4. How are you responding to these texts? Are you bored, fascinated, angry, excited, etc.? Why?

FIGURE 7.39

FREEDOM OF THE PRESS

FRIDAY JUNE 25 2010 *The Star*

They can't ban my mind, says cartoonist

KUALA LUMPUR: Malaysia has banned the work of three political cartoonists who criticise the government, but one of the artists said today that he was obligated to highlight issues other cartoonists would not.

The government said the cartoons in two books and a magazine posed a security threat.

Malaysia has banned dozens of publications in recent years, but usually because of sexual content or alleged misrepresentation ·

But the latest ban is certain to spark complaints that the government is not allowing critical views.

"All three publications have been banned for their contents that can influence the people to revolt against the leaders and government policies," said Home Ministry secretary-general Mahmood Adam.

"The contents are not suitable and are detrimental to public order."

The works are mainly by Zulkifli Anwar Ulhaque, known as Zunar, and other local cartoonists, questioning current events, such as police shootings and the sodomy trial of opposition leader Anwar Ibrahim.

The books, titled *Perak, Land of Cartoons* and *Funny Malaysia*, were published late last year. The magazine, Issues in Cartoons, was launched in February.

Zunar, 47, said he was still waiting for an official letter from the ministry but vowed not to stop drawing.

"The government is like this. They won't allow alternative views. You can do cartoons, you can do whatever artwork you want, but it must be in line with the government (view)," said Zunar, who has been a professional cartoonist for more than 20 years.

"Drawing cartoons is my social obligation... I will highlight the issues that Malaysian cartoonists have failed to highlight," he said. "They can ban my books, they can ban my publications, but they can't ban my mind." – Sapa-AP

FIGURE 7.40

Role play the meeting described below

The *Sunday Mail* is a widely read local newspaper. The editor has come under fire because their popular cartoonist has criticized public officials. At an editorial meeting, attended by the editor, the cartoonist, an advertiser and a reporter, there is disagreement about whether the controversial cartoonist should be censored or not. An angry government official who was recently lampooned by the cartoonist is also present at the meeting.

FIGURE 7.41 Zapiro cartoon

World sporting events require host countries to spend lots of money.

1. Who benefits? Who does not?

2. What is Zapiro's position? Should he be censored?

3. What sporting event is being shown? What has been built? What according to the cartoon could the money have been spent on? Who is 'committed' to what? Who says 'Huh! . . . Exactly!'?

Section 8: Digital technologies

The word technology comes from the Greek τεχνολογία (*technología*), from τέχνη (*téchnē*), meaning 'art, skill, craft', and -λογία (*-logía*), meaning 'study of'. As a discipline it is an applied science concerned with the knowledge and skill needed to invent and develop tools, machines and techniques in order to solve practical problems. 'Technologies' refers to the tools themselves that enable human beings to shape and change the physical world. Seen in this way, it is possible to think of the alphabet, paper, the ballpoint pen, the printing press, computers and the internet as technologies that have changed the way we are able to communicate.

People do not have equal access to technology. Technology may have changed our ability to move through space with the invention of motor vehicles, trains, aeroplanes and space ships but there are some people who cannot afford the bus fare to town. People are not equally mobile. Nor are they equally connected. It is significant that, while wealthier countries are concerned to ensure that everyone has access to the internet and computers, in poorer countries there are many people who have not yet had access to older technologies such as literacy or flush toilets.

Because technology has enabled human beings to shape and change the physical world, it is linked to power. It is worth pausing to think about the different technologies that give us a measure of control over our world and make our lives easier. Think about what it would be like to live without electricity, or running water, or transport, or refrigeration or penicillin. For many people this is their reality. It is worth making a list of all the technologies that you depend on daily to improve your quality of life. You might also like to think about technologies that do harm to people and to the planet.

Digital technologies have fundamentally transformed the communication landscape and are therefore the focus of this section. They impact on how we *do* literacy and why and how we need to *do* critical literacy. Before engaging with this section, you should consider the range of technologies available for communication and how they have changed the ways in which people produce and find information, how they send messages, how they stay in touch with their network of friends, how they organize revolutions, how they get news, how they do their homework, how they sell products and how they shop. You should then consider how literacy is implicated in all of this and why people need to be skilled text analysts.

Finally you need to think about the digital communication technologies that you and your friends have access to. Who owns them? What are they used for? Which technologies are the most desirable? Did you know that a 17-year-old Chinese teenager sold his kidney in order to buy an iPad and an iPhone? What sacrifices have you or your parents had to make to afford the technologies that you have access to? How does having your own tech stuff advantage you? Does your school have digital communication technologies? How have technologies made the production of multimodal texts easier than ever before?

As with the other sections in this book, this section can only introduce you to some of the key issues pertaining to digital technologies and questions of power, access, diversity and design. However, if this is something that interests you, it will provide you with many avenues to explore. Kerryn Dixon and Hilary Janks have tried to write it so that it will not be outdated before it is even published, a real danger given the speed of innovation. We have asked you to have some fun imagining what future communication technologies might look like.

The section begins with a focus on your access to technology and then asks you to consider what the different technologies enable. Pages 133–135 ask you to think about the infrastructure and the skills needed for access. You should log on to the interactive BBC website recommended on page 135 that allows you to see how access has changed over a decade.

Pages 136 and 137 explain and explore the differences between Web 1.0 and Web 2.0, and the key shift from users of the internet as consumers to producers of information. You need to plot your own use as a consumer and a producer, and you need to research and imagine what the future holds for internet users. The question of how networking has changed the nature of political action is discussed in the final section of the book. Some people argue that networking *is* Web 3.0 but you will need to do some research on how Web 3.0 is described. Some people fear that the future of the web will mean less personal freedom as governments use GPS technology to keep track of people.

There is already evidence that the internet poses a threat to print media: newspapers and magazines. This is another topic worthy of investigation and we would urge you to analyze the online print media campaign. We have been able to give you only a taste of the kind of arguments the magazine industry is making (p. 138). The actual advertisements bear closer analysis. See if you can work out how they contradict themselves.

Pages 136 to 137 deal with how these technologies have affected communication, language and imaging. Because they make it so easy to cut and paste and morph, we need to hone our critical literacy skills.

Finally this section deals with how these technologies are changing society. The issue of who owns and controls information is included for discussion as are issues of privacy and identity. The section covers interesting ground that invites you to read the age of digital communication critically and to play with new ideas. Some people argue that we are living through an age as profoundly disruptive as the industrial revolution. Some would even argue that machines have extended our physical capabilities so that we are now part human and part machine—cyborgs.

The section deals with questions of access and exclusion. In what ways are people without access to computers and other forms of digital technology disadvantaged? It invites you to think about technology as power over our environment and raises the threat of its misuse. It asks questions about the impact technology is having on our identities and it touches on the issue of identity theft. The section does not deal directly with design and redesign but this is implicit in the discussions of what these technologies enable us to do and how they make it easier to produce and redesign texts than ever before.

DIGITAL TECHNOLOGIES

FIGURE 8.1 iPad

FIGURE 8.2 Kindle

FIGURE 8.3 Flash drive

FIGURE 8.4 Digital camera

FIGURE 8.5 Scanner

The pictures on this page represent ten new technologies that students in 2012 would have seen or should know about.

1. What can each piece of technology do?

2. What does each piece of technology do best?

3. What old technology/ies did they replace?

4. What other technologies are there? What might they replace in the future?

5. What software does each technology need?

6. How portable is each piece of hardware?

7. Approximately how much does each item cost?

8. Which of these have you used?

9. Rank these technologies from least to most important for your life.

10. New technologies change very rapidly. What technologies do you think there will be in 2020 and what do you think they will be able to do?

FIGURE 8.6 PlayStation

FIGURE 8.7 Laptop

FIGURE 8.8 iPod

FIGURE 8.9 Smartphone

FIGURE 8.10 Smartboard

WHAT DIGITAL TECHNOLOGIES CAN DO

A concrete example of what a mobile phone enables you to do is that you can phone someone without having to be in a place where you have access to a fixed line. A limitation is that you have to be in an area that has a cell phone connection and you have to have airtime on your phone.

List other enabling and limiting features of mobile phones.

Work with a group. Each group should choose one of the other digital technologies discussed on the previous page. Consider the technology you have chosen in terms of its ability to

*   store different kinds of information
*   retrieve information
*   manipulate or redesign information
*   combine different kinds of information
*   communicate information
*   produce multimodal texts
*   interface with other technologies
*   move with you.

Report back to the class and compare your findings.

"We weren't compatible. I'm all Facebook while he's so Myspace."

FIGURE 8.11

FIGURE 8.12

? **The effects of new technologies** **?**
Research, consider, discuss

1. How have new technologies changed the way people interact socially?

2. How have new technologies changed the nature of work?

3. How have new technologies changed the communication landscape?

4. How have new technologies affected our health for better and for worse?

5. How have new technologies changed the way politics works?

ACCESS TO TECHNOLOGY

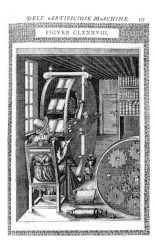

DELL' ARTIFICIOSE MACHINE. 317
FIGVRE CLXXXVIII.

The printing press was invented by Johannes Gutenberg in 1436. Because it reduced the price of printed materials, they became available for the masses to read. His press remained the standard until the 20th century.

Who do you think gets access to new technologies first? Who gets access last? Why?

FIGURE 8.13

Five centuries later approximately 1 billion people worldwide have not had access to literacy. Why?

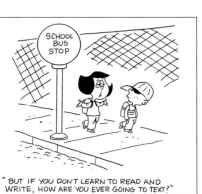

SCHOOL BUS STOP
" BUT IF YOU DON'T LEARN TO READ AND WRITE, HOW ARE YOU EVER GOING TO TEXT?"

FIGURE 8.14

What else does one need in the way of infrastructure, hardware, software and skills to become techno-literate?

What are the costs involved?

EXAMPLE (email)

- Infrastructure: electricity, telephone, service provider, bandwidth
- Hardware: computer, modem
- Software: Internet Explorer
- Skills: typing, ability to use email software
- Human resources: a resident geek.

The BBC provides an interactive map of the digital divide that shows the changes over a period of ten years. It can be found at site http://news.bbc.co.uk/1/hi/technology/8552410.stm.

FIGURE 8.15 Access to technology is changing all the time.

Unequal access to digital technologies is called *the digital divide*. The BBC map is a digital access indicator (DAI). This is worked out on the basis of

1. The number of fixed and mobile subscribers
2. The price of internet access
3. Adult literacy and school enrolment numbers
4. Quality of bandwidth
5. The number of internet users.

TASK

Study the map in order to explain the connection between access and relations of power.

THE INTERNET AND THE WORLD WIDE WEB 1.0

We can think of the internet as a huge library full of books. The rooms, corridors, ladders, shelves and all other infrastructure housing the books is the internet. The world wide web is like the books themselves. The books are the websites that make up the world wide web and the content of the books is the data on the web. A search engine is like a catalogue that uses key words to help you find the books and information you are looking for. The internet was invented by Tim Berners-Lee for the US military. When it was first opened to the public, the public used it largely to communicate by email and subsequently to access information. Some people call this stage of web use *Web 1.0*.

Can you think of other metaphors to describe the internet?

THE INFORMATION AGE

Because of its infinite capacity to store data, the world wide web has resulted in an explosion of information available at the tips of our fingers. Infinity is bigger than we can possibly imagine and without a good search engine we would never be able to find the information that we need.

To give you some idea of what it takes: In 2005, Google stored the world's information on more than 200,000 modified PCs. Now the number is closer to 2 million. Not only is the Google search engine the most powerful but also it is very user friendly. As a result all over the world people use the word *google* as a verb, meaning to conduct an internet search.

1. How can critical readers determine the accuracy and reliability of web content?

2. What is PageRank? How does it use quantity not quality as a sign of importance?

3. Find out how Google makes its money.

Did you know?

- Not all the information on the web is equally reliable.

- Which page comes up first when you do an internet search is not an accident.

- Other pop-ups are designed to tempt you to go elsewhere.

- The advertisements that come up for you are different from those that come up for other users.

THE INTERNET AND THE WORLD WIDE WEB 2.0

In Web 1.0 the public used the web largely to retrieve information. Web 2.0 is more interactive.

Web 2.0, the second phase of the WWW, enables users to

- produce, upload and change information
- connect through social networking sites
- share information quickly using new platforms
- access information in new ways
- store information in the cloud
- use other technologies besides the computer.

1.
Which of these sites do you use?

2.
Choose five of these sites that are new ones for you.

- What do they enable you to do?
- What are their limitations?

3.
Can you find one that no longer exists and suggest why?

4.
What have you uploaded on Web 2.0?

FIGURE 8.16

Source: http://cuip.uchicago.edu/~cac/ids/web2.0.jpg.

WHAT'S NEXT? > The web is about innovation! > Investigate Web 3.0. What is it? What are the concerns about it?

WILL THE WEB DESTROY PRINT MEDIA?

Since it became possible to access newspapers from around the world, the number of people buying newspapers has dropped dramatically. Most young people now get their news online instantly. Advertisers like pay-per-click advertising on the web. In the past, they had no way of directing their advertisements to the specific interests of potential buyers and they paid whether or not people read them. The web targets ads to users based on their browsing history. The internet could put traditional advertising companies out of business. The invention of the Kindle and Amazon's opening fixed price of $10 for an e-book is seen as a threat by publishers, who are hoping that competition for markets might save them. Five leading magazines mounted a multi-million dollar advertising campaign to 'tout the power of print' (*Wall Street Journal*, March 2010).

THE POWER OF PRINT CAMPAIGN   (http://powerofmagazines.com/)

The main argument of this campaign is that new media do not replace older media. Just as movies did not destroy radio, and television did not kill movies, the internet will not prevent people from buying and reading magazines. Different media coexist happily. The advertisements claim that magazines are stronger than ever. How do the headlines that they used in the campaign position magazines in relation to the internet?

We surf the internet.
We swim in magazines.

Will the internet kill magazines?
Did instant coffee kill coffee?

Google these to find the full text plus images.

- Do you read newspapers, books and magazines? Do you read them in print or online?
- Do you buy any of these media yourself?
- Would it matter if the print media disappeared? Why? Why not?
- If magazines are not worried, then why did they publish these advertisements?

Is text messaging destroying your use of the standard variety?

CHANGES IN THE WAYS WE COMMUNICATE

Once upon a time people used to buy notepaper and envelopes and stamps to send letters to people who lived down the road or on the other side of the world. Postmen used to collect these letters from shiny red postboxes and take them to the Post Office. There they would be sorted and sent to the person at the address on the envelope by road or sea or air. Depending on the mode of transport this could take a loooooooong time. By the time the letter arrived the information was often weeks old. In a world of email, text messaging, Facebook, Twitter and instant messaging, this all seems quaint, like fiction. Not so long ago people had to crank their telephones to get a shared line; now people go on-line and use video—Skype, which transmits sound and image instantly.

1. How are emails different from letters in language and content?
2. How are text messages different from email in language and content?
3. How are instant messages (like MXIT or BBM) different from text messages in language and content?
4. What are the distinguishing features of tweets?
5. Which of these do you use? Which of these do adults you know use? With whom? For what purpose? When? Who taught you?
6. Compare the answers given by men and women.

LANGUAGE AND NEW TECHNOLOGIES

Speech and writing are two different modes for making meaning. Here are some of the differences. Can you think of any others?

SPEECH	WRITING
oral	visual
face to face	at a distance
in the here and now	across time
less formal language: colloquial expressions, slang	more standard language: full sentences
incomplete sentences	grammatically correct, no abbreviations
known audience	known and unknown audiences
fleeting	permanent
clues from context and body language	content has to carry all of the message alone
clues from tone of voice	clues from punctuation, fonts and layout
clauses can be added to one another endlessly	clauses are more tightly related to one another
more use of co-ordinating conjunctions e.g. *and*, *or*, *but*	more use of subordinate conjunctions, e.g *if*, *as*
more repetition and hesitation that allows time for the speaker to think and the listener to follow.	tighter logic, structure and sequencing because the reader can go back if necessary.

TABLE 8.1

These differences are really at the ends of a continuum

Speech ⟵――――――――――――――――――――⟶ Writing

There are many genres that are part speech and part writing. For example, a politician may deliver a pre-written speech and a secretary might take minutes of what people say in a meeting. Where would you place the following mixed genres on this speech–writing continuum? Are they closer to speech or closer to writing?

- An instant message to your father to fetch you from a party
- A tweet about the results of a sports match
- An email to a teacher to arrange a meeting
- A message posted in a chat room about homework.

"But this is fantastic, professor! It's like no language I've ever seen before!"

FIGURE 8.17

1. Decipher the message in the cartoon.

2. Explain how to crack the code.

3. Who has access to the code? Who does not?

4. Why do people use it?

5. Will it survive?

6. Will it change standard language?

7. Is it subversive?

8. Is it affecting your own formal writing?

THE LANGUAGE OF NEW TECHNOLOGIES

Languages have closed and open sets of words. Pronouns, conjunctions, prepositions and articles are closed sets. This explains why feminist linguists were unable to introduce a non-sexist pronoun into the English language. Closed sets resist change and, as words with grammatical functions, they serve to keep the grammar of the language fairly stable. The open lexical sets, on the other hand—nouns, verbs, adjectives and adverbs—are dynamic. They allow for new ideas, contact with other languages and human creativity to keep the language movin' and shakin'.

New technologies have created the need for new terms. Words have had to be coined for new devices, new processes, new experiences. A whole new language. Create a new technologies dictionary. Use this example of a dictionary definition as a model.

Google (n) The name of a global internet company and its search engine.

google (v) to search for information on the internet. *If you don't know the meaning of a word just google it.*

Begin your dictionary by defining the words in the cloud tag below, then add additional terms that you know or encounter. TIP: You can make your own word cloud at www.wordle.net OR you can use old technologies to make a word collage by cutting words out of magazines.

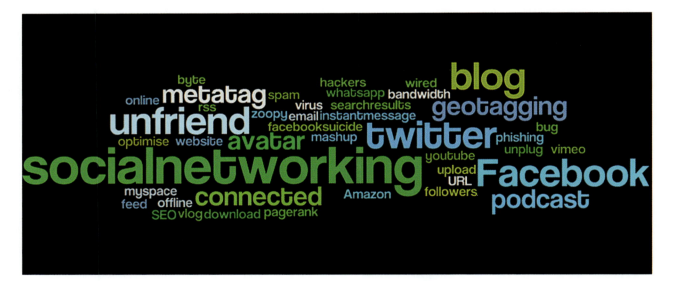

FIGURE 8.18

THE LANGUAGE OF THE INTERNET

Because the internet was developed in the US, English was for many years the dominant language on the web. This is changing. Find the latest figures for languages used on the web and discuss. The URL for world statistics is useful for this kind of information: www.internetworldstats.com.

DIGITAL MANIPULATION

Digital data is easy to play with. You can cut and paste and remix bits and pieces. The program Photoshop, which allows you to change images has, like Google, become a verb. The ease with which images can be changed means that images like words can be positioned to create particular effects. Critical viewers know that *seeing is not believing*. This is shown clearly by the Forbes advertisements with the tag line *Money makes you younger*.

FIGURE 8.19 Benjamin Franklin

Source: www.buzzfeed.com/copyranter/new-forbes-ads-claim-money-makes-you-look-youn.

FIGURE 8.20 President Andrew Jackson

Source: www.buzzfeed.com/copyranter/new-forbes-ads-claim-money-makes-you-look-youn.

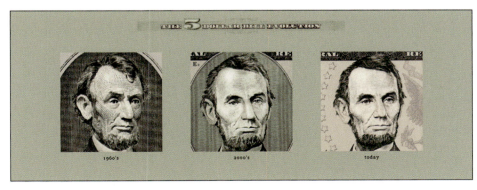

FIGURE 8.21 President Abraham Lincoln

Source: www.buzzfeed.com/copyranter/new-forbes-ads-claim-money-makes-you-look-youn.

1.
Why were the men given a makeover?

2.
What does this text say about social values in the US?

3.
According to this text what counts as masculine good looks?

4.
Explain what is meant by morphing. Describe what you use morphing for. Morph an image of your own face and describe the effect you have achieved.

5.
Take a picture of a celebrity and redesign it. Then get a classmate to discuss the effects of your redesign.

WHO OWNS INFORMATION? WHO CONTROLS INFORMATION?

 What does this symbol mean?

What kinds of texts do you find it on?

What does it suggest about the ownership of knowledge and information?

The ease with which one can cut, paste and remix digital data makes it easy for people to rip sound, image, print and video from the web.

What does this do to copyright?

© MUSIC

In the early 2000s Napster provided the technology that enabled people to share music as MP3 files. People were able to copy music for free. As a result of legal challenges for breaking © laws people are now supposed to pay for downloading music from the web. What Napster enabled music lovers to do was to access single songs rather than whole albums. This ultimately led to the selling of individual songs on iTunes.

NAPSTER—when the music's over you can turn out the lights.

© BOOKS

In 2004 Google announced its plan to digitize 15 million library books: 7 million from Michigan University, 1 million or more from Oxford University's nineteenth-century collection, 40,000 from Harvard, 12,000 from the New York Public Library and an unspecified number from Stanford. Not everyone was in favour of the book digitization project as it threatened the rights of authors and publishers. Copyrighted books would display only a few bits of text relating to a user's search and in a read-only form.

Go to Google Books. Look for a play by Shakespeare, a book by Lewis Carroll, a book by J. K. Rowling and a novel set for your English class.

1. How much of these books can you read on-line?
2. What happens when you try to print the book?
3. Who decides which parts of the book you can read?
4. If the whole book has been digitized who has control over this information? What are the consequences of this?

Google Books and Amazon, the largest on-line book seller, allow you to browse on-line. Napster went further and allowed you to download and save songs.

6. How has this affected the selling of books and music? How might it affect the selling of books and music in the future?
7. Who benefits?
8. How has it impacted on 20th-century notions of copyright?

WHAT'S PRIVATE? WHAT'S PUBLIC?

DISCUSSION

Do you like strangers to know where you have been? Do you want strangers to know where you have been on the internet? Do you want strangers to know what you like and dislike? Do you want strangers to know what you look like and who your friends and family are? Do you think adults worry too much about these things?

Analyze your friends' Facebook (or MySpace) pages

What content have they posted? What can a reader tell about them from this content? Who has access to their Facebook page? Who does not? What does this tell you about them? Have they posted photographs? Who is in the photographs? Have any people in the photographs been tagged? Do the people in the photographs know they are on this Facebook page? Have they given permission to have their image posted here? Do your friends know how to remove this information?

Facebook and other networking sites keep changing their privacy settings, which affects how much of your information can be accessed in the public domain. Have you read the privacy settings? What do they say? Do you know how to change them? In the light of this and your answers to your analysis of a friend's page, what would you change on your page?

Who knows where you have been? Do you care? What's at stake?
Did you know that Google is constantly trawling the web for information and that it spies on your on-line browsing habits? Did you know that Amazon tracks your browsing habits and the kinds of books and products you have shown an interest in? Tracking tells them what your interests are so that they can send you personalized adverts. They also know where other people like you have been and what they buy, and they share this information with you to entice you to buy more. 'Other people who bought this book also bought . . .'

How much information do these and other companies have about you? What do you think should be private and what can be shared? What if 'homeland security' subpoenaed this information?

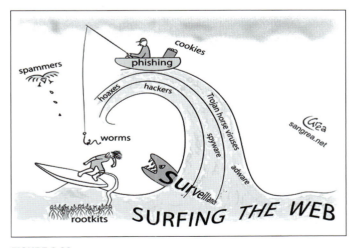

FIGURE 8.22

Source: www.sangrea.net.

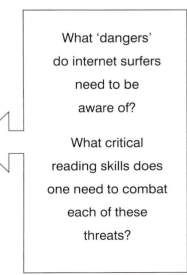

What 'dangers' do internet surfers need to be aware of?

What critical reading skills does one need to combat each of these threats?

CYBORG IDENTITIES

Cyborg is short for *cybernetic organism*, which in the case of human beings has come to be thought of as someone who is part human and part machine. Cyborgs have abnormal abilities that have been enhanced by technology. Outside of science fiction, it is interesting to consider the extent to which we are dependent on machines to extend the limitations of our own bodies—heart monitors for sports training; cars instead of legs for travelling; aeroplanes to fly; computers to find and share information; iPods for listening to music; mobile devices to keep us connected. Cyberspace is the virtual world in which we move and GPS navigation systems make sure that we do not get lost when we return to the real world. We have already seen how our movement can be tracked in cyberspace. The fear is that GPS will enable others to keep track of us in our everyday lives.

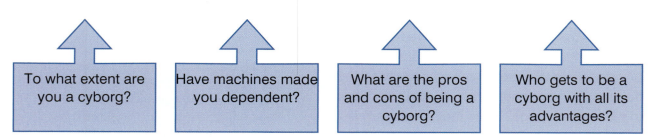

| To what extent are you a cyborg? | Have machines made you dependent? | What are the pros and cons of being a cyborg? | Who gets to be a cyborg with all its advantages? |

Examine the Turkish Airlines portrait of Kobe Bryant, a 205 pound, six foot six basketball player.

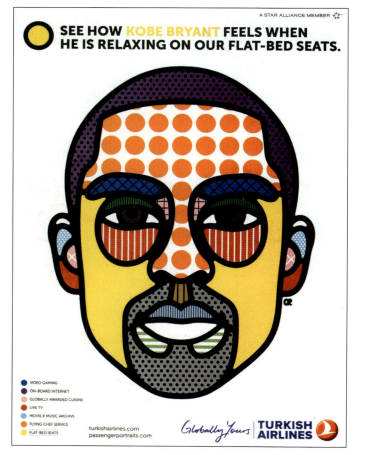

FIGURE 8.23

1. Examine the key carefully in order to decode the portrait. How has Kobe Bryant been portrayed?

2. How has relaxation been constructed verbally and visually?

3. What is the effect of representing Kobe Bryant as a disembodied head?

4. Discuss flat-bed seats in relation to the distribution of space and bodies on aeroplanes. Who is excluded altogether?

5. Kobe Bryant has been portrayed as a cyborg. Which parts are human and which parts are machine?

> Using the Turkish Airlines passenger portraits as a model, draw your own portrait as a cyborg.

Section 9: Redesign—from critical literacy to social action

Section 9 and its introduction were written by Hilary Janks. It works with redesign in a different way. Here we are not simply redesigning texts, but reshaping the social world by transformative social action.

Since Paulo Freire taught literacy as a means for people to liberate themselves by problematizing their worlds in order to change them, critical literacy has been linked to the ideal of social emancipation. If all critical literacy could achieve was awareness, without developing peoples' agency—their ability to act in the face of discrimination, inequality or abuse—then it might simply produce despair. Critical literacy has been called 'a pedagogy of hope', because it believes in our ability to transform the conditions in which we find ourselves.

Imagine discovering when you apply for a driver's licence that you have no legal right to be living in the country you call home because your documents are fake. This is what happened to Jose Antonio Vargas. He is one of an estimated 11.5 million people living in the United States as undocumented migrants. Many of these came as young children, were educated in the US and now work and pay taxes while living in constant fear of discovery and deportation. In June 2011 Vargas 'came out' as an undocumented immigrant against the advice of immigration lawyers. His action was the first in what has become a movement with more than 2,000 others outing themselves in the course of the next year. As Vargas 'a Philippines-born, college educated, outspoken, mainstream journalist' discovered, coming out has, ironically, protected him. He describes the role played by social media in this movement, which has its own Facebook page, United We Dream, and a series of videos on YouTube, *Undocumented and Awkward* (*Time*, 23 June 2012).

Now, if you google 'Vargas', you get over 6 million hits. His action led the way for others and has highlighted the plight of the 'Dreamers' named after the Dream Act immigration bill, which has yet to be passed in the US. It is immensely brave to be the first person to speak out, to embrace all the uncertainty of a decision that one of his lawyers described as 'legal suicide'. But it also takes courage for others to take this step. This is an example of a situation in which big *P* politics is shown to have little *p* consequences in people's everyday lives, in which the political is intensely personal.

The term 'coming out' was borrowed from the gay rights movement, another social movement that has enabled people to own their identities in the face of discrimination on the basis of their sexual orientation.

Social action is not always as public as this or as personally dangerous. Vargas describes how many ordinary American citizens, pastors, teachers and good Samaritans protect young undocumented migrants, making their lives easier. Quietly, these people have taken a stand.

Have you ever come away from a situation where you witnessed or were subjected to unfair treatment or abuse wishing you had acted or responded differently? How often have the words you should have said come to you much later? None of these experiences should be wasted because invariably you will be given another chance. Someone else will be victimized in your presence or, having succeeded in putting you down once, your tormentor will try again.

But if you problematize the moments when you missed the opportunity to deal with a situation, you will be ready next time. Critical literacy is as much about 'reading' our daily encounters with others as it is about reading our own behavior and reactions. While we cannot control how others behave, we can control what we do. This understanding is in and of itself empowering because we can begin to see ourselves as having agency.

We can exercise our agency for good or ill: we can empower ourselves at the expense of others or work for a more just and humane society. Often it is small things that can make a difference to someone else's life. A principal of a poor school taught me that the things I discard could be used in her school, so I began to collect and deliver my useful 'rubbish'. In the process I learnt that my garbage was an indication of my privileged life. You should try reading your garbage critically. How much of it could be recycled or re-used?

In order to take action one has to be able to name the problem. This section gives examples of school projects related to small *p* social action and of *cyberactivism.* Cyberactivism uses the internet to effect change. You are invited to explore three examples in which ordinary people have used the internet to intervene in the realm of big *P* politics.

Taking literally Paulo Freire's injunction to read the word and the world, this section shows how thinking globally can enable us to act locally. Here global warming is used as an example of naming a problem so that action can follow. Living greener lives is something that ordinary people can undertake in order to protect the planet. Here individual action can contribute to collective action on a much larger scale.

Because climate change results from our actions that have interfered with nature the section moves to a discussion of *nature* and what is natural. How we construct what is natural is at the heart of the process of naturalization, one of the modes of power identified by Thompson and discussed in Section 1. Here the example used is the way in which the nuclear family has been naturalized as the norm. In reality many children live in large, extended families, in small single-parent families or in two different families after a divorce.

Because this is the last section of the book, it has two concluding activities. These are unusual in that they invite you to reflect critically on this book, *Doing Critical Literacy*, using the skills you have acquired.

FROM CRITICAL AWARENESS TO SOCIAL ACTION

Paulo Freire is a famous Brazilian educator who made his mark by linking literacy education in Brazil to political action. He was the first to coin the term *critical literacy*. He argued that reading the word was important for reading the wor*l*d.

'To exist, humanly, is to *name* the world, to change it. Once named, the world in its turn reappears to its namers as a problem and requires of them a new *naming*. . . . It is in speaking their word that men transform the world by naming it.'

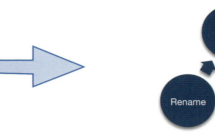

FIGURE 9.1 Freire's redesign cycle

Examples of renaming or redesigning activities already included in this workbook	
p. 14	Re-drawing the world to challenge maps based on Europe as the centre of the world.
p. 30	Changing the point of view: My parents kept me from children like Stephen Spender.
p. 45	Re-naming Americans to challenge Western versions of so-called primitive "others".
p. 49	Re-writing the outcome of The Music Lesson.
p. 51	Re-naming oneself or one's group.
p. 120	Adbusters' culture jamming.

Find other examples.

Now find examples of texts that you have deconstructed and redesign them.

Wangari Muta Maathai, known in Kenya as 'the tree woman', established the Green Belt Movement in Kenya. This movement assisted women in planting more than 20 million trees on their farms and on schools and church compounds in order to conserve the environment. The movement grew to include projects to preserve biodiversity, educate people about their environment and promote the rights of women and girls. For this Wangari Maathai was awarded a Nobel Prize (adapted from http://nobelprize.org and http://news.bbc.co.uk/2/hi/africa/3726024.stm).

FIGURE 9.2

Research project

Find other examples of collective action that have made a difference to people's lives or to the environment.

MAKING A DIFFERENCE

Many critical literacy projects around the world involve students making a difference, however small, to their schools, neighbourhoods and communities. The projects included here all used literacy as a form of action. This included a range of literacy genres: letters, surveys, petitions, plans, records, stories, poems.

Paulina Sethole named hunger as a problem in her school and, with the help of BMW, the parents, teachers and children, established a sustainable food garden and a feeding scheme. For BMW, sustainable development was a problem that they could contribute to 'renaming'.

FIGURE 9.3

Literacy researchers at the University of South Australia, working with teachers, provided young people from the Murray-Darling Basin with opportunities to develop new knowledge about their local places and to become involved in communication about the care, and the improvement, of their environment.

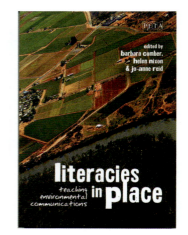

FIGURE 9.5

Ernest Morrell's projects in the US enabled young people to produce a wide range of texts in different media that engaged with a range of social issues. These included, amongst others, the quality of education in urban schools, cyberactivism and the role of the media in the 2000 Democratic Convention.

FIGURE 9.4

Patricia Watson worked with students to produce *Heart to Heart*, a comic divided into three parts that invites readers to consider two parallel stories about young people confronted with pressure to have sex. Between the stories, the comic shows the process that enabled the first story to be reconstructed.

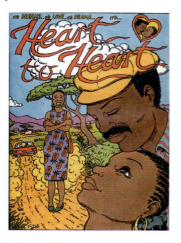

FIGURE 9.6

What problem can you tackle collectively to make a difference where you live?

CYBERACTIVISM

The internet is a powerful tool for collective social action. It includes using the internet to

- organize actions such as protests, petitions, fundraising
- create awareness and mobilize support for a cause
- create interaction where people can contribute their ideas and their responses.

Communication technologies such as Twitter, Facebook, email, Chat, YouTube and podcasts are faster, cheaper and more interactive ways of sharing information with large audiences. Access to information is more democratic because anyone with access to the internet can produce or forward ideas to others. Up-to-the-minute news spreads rapidly and the authorities no longer have the power to censor or control it.

FIGURE 9.7 Social networking sites for cyberactivism

Research project

Choose an example of cyberactivism that interests you and analyze it using critical literacy questions.

1. Make an assessment of its overall aims and effects.
   - Work out whose interests are served, who benefits, who is disadvantaged. Decide whether it works to maintain or resist existing relations of power. Is it worthy of support? Will the cause make a difference to people's lives?
2. Make an assessment of its audience.
   - Who is included? Who is excluded? Who speaks and who is silenced? Who speaks for whom? How is online participation encouraged? Who is heard? Does it speak to you or your peer group?
3. Make an assessment of its messages.
   - How are the messages designed to appeal to their audience? Are they multimodal? What communication technologies are used? How might the message be redesigned to be more effective?
4. Decide as a class what social action online might be worth supporting.

Famous examples of cyberactivism for you to investigate and analyze critically

The Arab Spring	Wikileaks	Occupy Wall Street
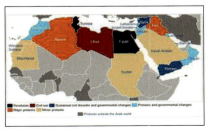		

FIGURE 9.8 The Arab Spring, Wikileaks, Occupy Wall Street

READING THE WORLD

When Freire taught literacy in Brazil, he wanted his adult learners to 'read' their own social context in order to improve the conditions under which they worked and lived. Today the world is a more connected place as a result of globalization. One of the required outcomes for education in South Africa is that students should develop 'an understanding of the world as a set of related systems by understanding that problem-solving contexts do not exist in isolation'.

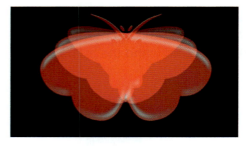

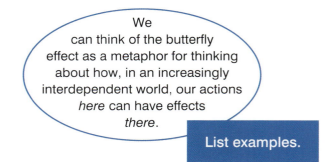

We can think of the butterfly effect as a metaphor for thinking about how, in an increasingly interdependent world, our actions *here* can have effects *there*.

List examples.

FIGURE 9.9 The butterfly effect—a metaphor

Did you know that a single flap of a butterfly's wings in Brazil can generate a tornado in Texas? This discovery of Lorenz, a meteorologist who maps weather patterns, is known as the butterfly effect.

THINK GLOBAL ACT LOCAL

How, in small ways, can each of us help to make the world a better place for everyone?

Wangari Maathai provides us with an example.

The removal of forests is an environmental concern in poor countries around the world. When Wangari Maathai began her work, she set up a local tree-planting project that was designed to empower local women by giving them skills that would benefit them and their communities while simultaneously contributing to saving the local environment and the planet.

(www.greenbeltmovement.org)

FIGURE 9.10

Can you give other examples of thinking global and acting local?

KNOWLEDGE BEFORE ACTION

CLIMATE CHANGE AS AN EXAMPLE

Climate change is a good example of a global situation where each one of us could make a local contribution.

Before we can make a contribution we need to understand what causes climate change. This will enable us to make decisions about what we can do.

WE NEED KNOWLEDGE in order

- to understand climate change and how it has been named and described (i.e. constructed/represented)
- to recognize climate change as a problem and to understand the nature of the problem—who benefits and who is disadvantaged by the different namings?
- to know how to act in order to make a difference.

NAMING, PROBLEMATIZING AND RENAMING ALL REQUIRE KNOWLEDGE.

Research

Find out enough to agree or disagree with the statements alongside. You should be able to defend your position.

What could you do to make a difference?

Burning fossil fuels releases greenhouse gases (GHGs), which cause climate change.

The removal of forests causes climate change. Trees are called 'the lungs of the world' because they soak up carbon dioxide and release oxygen.

Climate change is causing species of animals and plants to become extinct.

Reduce Reuse Recycle

Global warming is causing the glaciers to melt and oceans to rise. This is a threat to low-lying countries.

Climate scientists agree that a rise in surface temperature of more than 2° Celsius would be a disaster for the planet and for human beings.

Tsunamis, hurricanes and cyclones are a consequence of global warming.

If we fail to act now the results will be catastrophic.

Climate change is part of a natural cycle.

MAKING A DIFFERENCE TO CLIMATE CHANGE

If everyone were to reduce the amount of carbon dioxide they emit into the atmosphere, then collectively we could reduce the world's carbon emissions and help to save the planet. To do so, we need to know how to measure our carbon footprint and how to reduce it.

> If you have an internet connection there are several websites that will measure your carbon footprint, once you have entered some information. The coolest and simplest website is the Kids Carbon Footprint Calculator as the questions are more geared to young people's life-style (travelling to school, watching TV, etc.) See www.cooltheworld.com/kidscarboncalculator.php. What it comes down to is that if you *reduce* what you consume, *reuse* goods and *recycle* your waste, you will have a lower carbon footprint.

GO GREEN

10 ways to save energy, with one example for each suggestion. Can you give other examples? How many other ways to save energy can you think of? Make a list and give examples.

1. Save energy	(Set your thermostat a few degrees lower in the winter).
2. Save water to save money	(Take shorter showers to reduce water).
3. Use less gas	(Walk or bike to work).
4. Eat smart	(Whatever your diet, eat low on the food chain).
5. Don't drink bottled water	(Bring a reusable water bottle, preferably aluminium when you are not at home).
6. Think before you buy	(When making purchases, make sure you know what's "Good Stuff" and what isn't).
7. Borrow instead of buying	(Borrow from libraries instead of buying personal books and movies).
8. Buy smart	(Buy in bulk. Purchasing food from bulk bins can save money and packaging).
9. Keep electronics out of the trash	(Recycle your cell phone).
10. Make your own cleaning supplies.	(You can make non-toxic cleaning supplies from baking soda, vinegar, lemon, and soap).
** Bonus Item!	(Stay informed about going green).

MAKING A DIFFERENCE TO THE WORLD FROM THE GLOBAL TO THE LOCAL
The global threat to the environment requires everyone to work together locally to save the planet. How can you personally contribute to saving the world with all its bio-diversity?

MAKING A DIFFERENCE TO YOUR WORLD FROM THE LOCAL TO THE GLOBAL
What worries you about your own local context? Name the problem and decide what you can do about it and who else you could involve (e.g. consumerism, littering, no recycling).

GREENPEACE

Research project

Find an answer to this question:

Why did Al Gore and his team of scientists win a *peace* prize for their work on climate change?

FIGURE 9.11

Greenpeace is an independent global campaigning organisation that acts to change attitudes and behaviour, to protect and conserve the environment and to promote peace by:

1. **Catalysing an energy revolution** to address the number one threat facing our planet: climate change.
2. **Defending our oceans** by challenging wasteful and destructive fishing, and creating a global network of marine reserves.
3. **Protecting the world's ancient forests** and the animals, plants and people that depend on them.
4. **Working for disarmament and peace** by tackling the causes of conflict and calling for the elimination of all nuclear weapons.
5. **Creating a toxic free future** with safer alternatives to hazardous chemicals in today's products and manufacturing.
6. **Campaigning for sustainable agriculture** by rejecting genetically engineered organisms, protecting biodiversity and encouraging socially responsible farming.
   (**www.greenpeace.org**)

Are all of these related to world peace? If so, how?

The internet is full of articles about climate change, with writers expressing a wide range of views. The main line of disagreement has to do with whether global warming is natural or the result of human actions. What is at stake in this argument is whether or not we need to change our behavior. Critical literacy can help us to recognize the different positions taken up in these articles, but in order to make up our own minds we all need some basic scientific literacy.

Food for thought

Who has access to basic scientific literacy?
Why is this important for democratic citizenship?
In relation to this issue, how are reading the *word* and reading the *world* connected?
What are the little *p* politics of this issue and what are the big *P* politics?
Which big businesses have vested interests in how we understand global warming?
Which businesses are investing in climate change research? Why?

NATURE AND NATURALIZATION

Collocation: Words that are used together regularly are said to collocate. Collocation invites us to think about words that are associated with one another. So, for example, when Tony Blair said that Britain needed to join Bush in his war against Iraq he said that it was necessary because 'Sadam Hussein is a serial (pause) breaker of promises' (BBC World News). The pause allowed just enough time for the listener to fill in the word that we usually associate with the word 'serial'. Collocation is a linguistic feature that gives us access to what is often unsaid.

> Make a list of words that collocate with the words *nature* and *natural*.

Explain these concepts and binaries. Give examples and discuss which terms are viewed positively and which are viewed negatively.

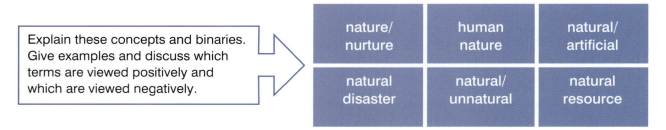

nature/nurture	human nature	natural/artificial
natural disaster	natural/unnatural	natural resource

There is a great deal at stake in how we decide what is and is not part of nature.

Here are some examples.

Homophobes say that homosexuality is unnatural.

Caster Semenya, a middle-distance runner and world champion, was subjected to gender testing because her testosterone levels were deemed by sports officials to be unnaturally high for a woman.

The Baby Book (Sears, 1993, 2005) says that mothers and babies evolved to be close to each other. Nature is therefore used to support the practice of attachment parenting and arguments that mothers should stay at home to rear their children.

Can you find other examples?

NATURALIZATION

Naturalization is one of Thompson's modes of operation of ideology discussed on page 29. If we name something as natural—as part of nature—then we tend to think of it as inevitable and unchangeable, so there is not a need for us to act. For example, it is natural for the world to rotate around the sun and for the moon to cause the tides.

However, we often construct things as natural so that people will *think* that there is nothing we can do about them and nothing we should have done to prevent them. For example, there is little disagreement about global warming. The disagreement is about whether the causes are natural or a result of people's actions. Here is another example: Men cannot breast feed children. That is a fact of nature. The conclusion drawn from this fact, that men cannot look after children, is a cultural belief, not a fact of nature. The social construction of men's and women's roles based on biological differences led feminists to (re)name this way of thinking as 'sexist' and as 'gendered'.

MAKING A DIFFERENCE TO THE WAY WE THINK

Naturalization is a powerful force. It constructs our sense of what is normal based on how our communities see and name the world. We forget that what is natural for us is not natural or normal for everyone. This often leads to intolerance and to seeing other people's behavior as unnatural or deviant. Do the activities below. They are designed to change your taken-for-granted ways of thinking. What action could result from this?

Discuss the family structures shown in these pictures.

FIGURE 9.12 Public domain images

If you google images of families or cartoon families on the internet, the images below are the kinds of image that you get. What does this tell us? To find different kinds of family structures you have to specify, e.g. 'same sex families', or 'single parent families'. What do these naming practices tell us?

FIGURE 9.13 Public domain images

Define *family*.

List the members of your family and their relationship to you (e.g. sister, mother). English may not have words for a particular relationship. If so, use the word in your home language for the relationship.

Draw your family tree. Try to include three or four generations.

Compare the family structures of members of your class and discuss the family structures shown in these pictures.

FAMILIES, PRIVILEGE AND OPPORTUNITY

Answer these questions about yourself.

1. Can you read and write?
2. Are you computer literate?
3. Do you have internet access at home?
4. Do you have internet access at school?
5. Is your home language the language used at school?
6. Did your parents finish school?
7. Did your parents go to university?
8. How many books are there at home?
9. Do you own any books?
10. Does your family buy a daily newspaper?
11. Does your family buy magazines?
12. Is there someone at home who can help you with your homework?
13. Do you have a cell phone?
14. Does your family have a TV?
15. Does your family have a radio?
16. How many breadwinners are there in your family and how many people do they have to feed and clothe?
17. Do you have your own room?
18. Does your family own a car?
19. Does your home have running water?
20. Does your home have electricity?

WHO GETS ACCESS TO WHAT RESOURCES IS AN IMPORTANT CRITICAL LITERACY QUESTION

Who do you think gets access to new technologies first? Arrange the groups below in order from least likely to most likely. There are no right answers. It is the discussion that is important. The discussion deals with the relationship between access and social differences.

How privileged do you think you are?

If you are at school and working through this book, then already you have had access to education and to literacy that many other young people have been denied.

It is important to remember that success in life is usually related to the opportunities people have had.

How can one use one's privilege responsibly to pay back to society?

Research activity

Collect images of families that are used to sell products. You will find them in advertisements, on packaging and in brochures.

1. What kinds of products use pictures of families? Why?
2. What kinds of families are chosen? Why?
3. What does this say about which families are normal and which are not?

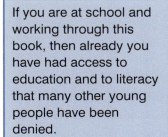

American	poor	black	Asian	young	European
African	disabled	unschooled	rural	white	old
able-bodied	educated	males	rich	females	urban

FIGURE 9.14

CONCLUSION—CAN YOU TELL A BOOK BY ITS COVER?

Below you will find two Routledge titles written by Janks and Dixon. Each title has a different cover for the softcover and hardcover books.

1. Which would you rather read? Why?

2. Use your critical visual literacy skills to analyze these covers.

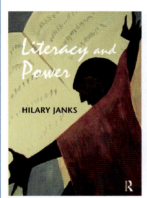

FIGURE 9.15

FIGURE 9.16

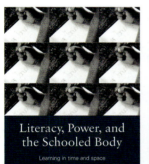

FIGURE 9.17

FIGURE 9.18

Now look carefully at the cover of this book by Jerome Harste in order to do a critical visual analysis.

- You should pay attention to the images, the words and the fonts.
- You should explain the intertextual references to *Literacy and Power* and consider the reasons for these references.
- How does this cover relate to the issues of power, identity and difference, access and design?

For many years Jerry Harste's students have produced images of literacy and power in the style of Jacob Lawrence, a famous American Civil Rights artist. These images as well as the image used for *Literacy and Power* were produced by teachers in Jerry Harste's courses at the University of Indiana.

FIGURE 9.19

FIGURE 9.20

FIGURE 9.21

FIGURE 9.22

FIGURE 9.23

Each of these images was considered for the cover of this book.

- Would any of these images have been better for the cover of *Doing Critical Literacy?* Why? Why not?
- How do these images relate to the issues of power, identity and difference, access and design, that are central concerns of the book?
- Redesign the cover of this book to make a better statement of what doing critical literacy entails.

CRITICAL LITERACY ANALYSIS OF *DOING CRITICAL LITERACY*

The central argument of this book is that all texts are positioned by the writer and they work to position the reader. If this is so, then this book, *Doing Critical Literacy*, is also a text that has worked to position you. In this final activity, you are invited to produce a critical reading of the different sections of this book and of the book as a whole.

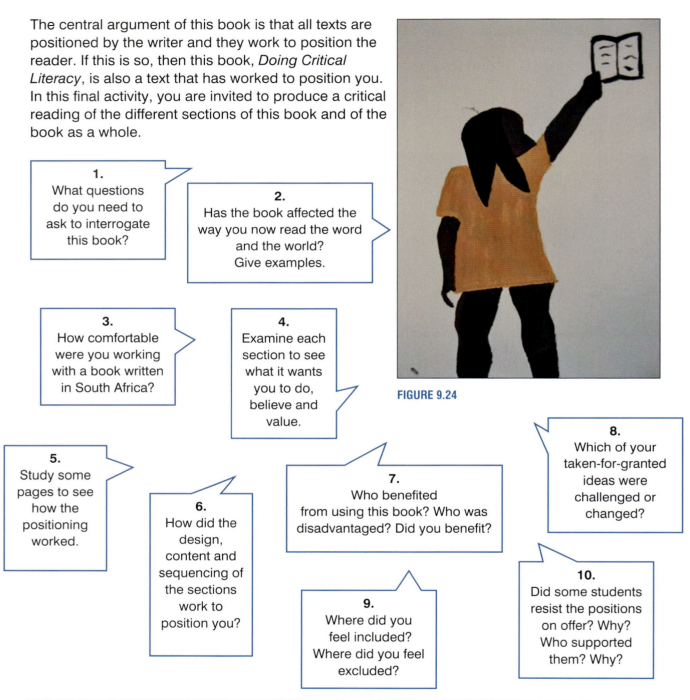

FIGURE 9.24

1.
What questions do you need to ask to interrogate this book?

2.
Has the book affected the way you now read the word and the world? Give examples.

3.
How comfortable were you working with a book written in South Africa?

4.
Examine each section to see what it wants you to do, believe and value.

5.
Study some pages to see how the positioning worked.

6.
How did the design, content and sequencing of the sections work to position you?

7.
Who benefited from using this book? Who was disadvantaged? Did you benefit?

8.
Which of your taken-for-granted ideas were challenged or changed?

9.
Where did you feel included? Where did you feel excluded?

10.
Did some students resist the positions on offer? Why? Who supported them? Why?

How successful was this book in helping you to understand the relationship between language and power, language and identity, language and access, language and social transformation? How successful was it in helping you to recognize that power, identity, access and design are all interconnected and need to be accounted for in designing and redesigning texts?

Notes

1. Sonia Nieto happens to be the editor of the series in which this book is published.

2. So oft in theologic wars,
   The disputants, I ween,
   Rail on in utter ignorance
   Of what each other mean,
   And prate about an Elephant
   Not one of them has seen!

   This is the moral of the elephant poem by John Godfrey Saxe. It means that the arguments between the six men are based on ignorance about an elephant that none of them has seen.

3. Useful rules for classroom debates can be found on the web at www.edu.gov.mb.ca/k12/cur/socstud/frame_found_sr2/tns/tn-13.pdf.

4. The *Time* caption for the Obama portrait by Dylan Roscover was, 'Obama, burdened. The president took power at a time of crisis. How can he recover his stride?' (*Time*, Volume 175, No. 4, 1 February 2010, p. 10).

5. Try reading the word 'Nacirema' backwards.

6. For the full speech go to www.billcosbypoundcakespeech.htm.

7. In July 2009, Henry Louis Gates, Jr., Harvard University professor, was arrested at his home in Cambridge, Massachusetts by a local police officer responding to a 9 1-1 caller's report of men breaking and entering the residence.

8. Translations of local words in *Joe's Beat* in the order in which they appear:

   Tyini, unzima, lomthwalo—a heavy burden; mpintshi—my friend; broer—brother; mala mogudu—tripe; atchaar—spicy Indian relish; skaapkop—sheep's head; machangaan wors—sausage made by Shangaans (an African tribe); chibuku—beer; mageu—sorghum beer; scamptho—the slang spoken by youth in urban African townships in South Africa with words from a range of South African languages; kwaito—a type of music originating from South Africa; hood—short for neighbourhood; arme darkie—poor dark person; Ziyamporoma—an expression of delight; amagents—township slang for flashy young men; jitas—cool dudes; pap—porridge; tsotsi taal—another name for scamtho. A tsotsi is a gangster and scamtho was formerly spoken by shady youth, but it is now much more widespread; fly ghetto laaitie—streetwise youngster; mtshana—my friend; umkhukumtsha—interpreters; morogo—wild spinach; stokvels—informal communal money-saving groups; tebellos—night vigils; amadlozi ceremonies—ancestor ceremonies; mgosi—liquor; the nose brigade—people who speak with a posh nasalized accent; kitchen girl—domestic worker; they 'hi' and 'what's-up' the arme ouma—they speak to their grandmothers in a very informal and therefore culturally disrespectful way; nogal—moreover; Laf' elihle kakhulu madoda—Cry the beloved country (a reference to a book by Alan Paton about life in South Africa).

9. Aardvark: Afrikaans (some might argue Dutch).
   Bungalow: Hindi (and Bengali).
   Chocolate: Nahuatl (language of the Aztecs).
   Economy: Ancient Greek.
   Ghoul: Arabic.
   Gimmick: This is contested. It could be Irish, Gaelic or German.
   Ignoramus: Latin.
   Mosquito: Spanish.
   Parachute: French.
   Saga: Old Norse.
   Tycoon: Japanese.
   Zombie: Kikongo (West African).

10. For the history of Santa Claus and Coca-Cola see www.thecoca-colacompany.com/heritage/cokelore_santa.html.

11. *Buy.ology* (Lindstrom, 2008).

References

Anonymous. (1956, April). Death in the dark city, *Drum*.

Anonymous. (2006, May). Tres jeans. *SL*, p. 38.

Anonymous. (2007). The ten ways *Star Wars* changed the movie industry. Movie merchandising. Downloaded 26 November 2012, www.time.com/time/specials/2007/article/0,28804,1625074_1625073_1625067,00.html.

Anonymous. (2010, 5 March). Royals shock Zuma, *Mail and Guardian*.

Anonymous. (2010, 24 March). The filth of Fleet Street, *Star*.

Anonymous. (2010, 19 April). Boys will be boys, and girls will love their dolls. *Star*.

Anonymous. (2012, 3 March). Move over brother. *Economist*. Downloaded 26 November 2012, www.economist.com/node/21548976.

Anonymous. Good hair. Sundance film festival archives. Downloaded 26 November 2012, http://history.sundance.org/films/5655.

Anonymous. (n.d.). Columbine high school massacre. Downloaded 26 November 2012, http://en.wikipedia.org/wiki/Columbine_High_School_massacre.

Bacevich, J. (2008). He told us to go shopping. Now the bill is due. *Washington Post*. Downloaded 26 November 2012, www.washingtonpost.com/wp-dyn/content/article/2008/10/03/AR2008100301977.html.

Bauer, A. (2010, 8 February). Verbatim, *Time*.

Biko, S. (1976, May). SASO/BPC Trial.

Bird, C. (1998). *The Stolen Children*. New South Wales: Random House.

Blommaert, J. (2008). *Grassroots Literacy*. London: Routledge.

Blommaert, J. (2010). *The Sociolinguistics of Globalization*. Cambridge: Cambridge University Press.

Bullock, L. (2006). Testers posing as Katrina survivors encounter 'linguistic profiling'. NNPA news report. Downloaded 26 November 2012, http://news.newamerica media.org/news/view_ article.html?article_id=88d97b82640f6ba16f5e07d9d695a1b3.

Christensen L. (2000). *Reading, Writing and Rising Up*. Milwaukee: Rethinking Schools.

Cosby, B. (2004). We have got to take the neighbourhood back. Downloaded 26 November 2012, www.quotesstar.com/quotes/w/weve-got-to-take-the-28961.html.

Finney, J. in P. Straub (ed.). (2009). *American Fantastic Tales: Terror and the Uncanny from the 1940s until Now*. New York: Library of America.

Freebody, P. and Luke, A. (1990). Literacies programmes: debates and demands in cultural contexts. *Prospect: A Journal of Australian TESOL* 11, 7–16.

Freire, P. (1972a). *Cultural Action for Freedom*. Harmondsworth: Penguin.

Freire, P. (1972b). *Pedagogy of the Oppressed*. Harmondsworth: Penguin.

Foucault, M. (1970). The order of discourse. Inaugural Lecture at the College de France. In M. Shapiro (ed.). *Language and Politics*. Oxford: Basil Blackwell.

Gee, J. (1990). *Social Linguistics and Literacies*. London: Falmer Press.

Gobhozi, A. (2010, 7 September). I thought SA media was bad.

Herman, J. (1983). I am what I am. Downloaded 2 November 2012, http://lyrics.doheth.co.uk/.

Hymes, D. (1972) On communicative competence. In J. Pride and J. Holmes. *Sociolinguistics*. Harmondsworth: Penguin.

Isaacson, W. (2011) *Steve Jobs*. New York: Simon & Schuster.

Janks, H. (2010). *Literacy and Power*. London and New York: Routledge.

Jones, R. (1990). Reader, writer, text. In R. Carter, (ed.). *Knowledge about Language and the Curriculum.* London: Hodder & Stoughton.

Klein, N. (1999). *No Logo.* New York: Picador.

Lindstrom, M. (2008). *Buy.ology.* New York: Doubleday.

Malala, J. (2012, 27 May). Why Malindi cried. *Sunday Times Review.*

Miner, H. (1956). Body ritual among the Nacirema. *American Anthropologist*, 58, 3, 503–507.

Ngũgĩ wa Thiong'o. (1991). *Decolonising the Mind.* Nairobi: James Currey & Heinemann.

Niemöller, M. (1937). Quotation downloaded 2 November, 2012, www.ushmm.org/wlc/en/article.php?ModuleId=10007392.

Political staff. (1986, 21 March). 1985 had at least 1,000 'Chameleons'. *Star.*

Readers' views. (2010, 5 March). SMSs. *Star.*

Rock, C. (n.d.). Downloaded 26 November 2012, http://thinkexist.com/quotation/yeah-i_love_being_famous-it-s_almost_like_being/304328.html.

Rosen, M. (2004). Chivvy. Downloaded 2 November 2012, www.withamstaple.com/GArchive/DArchivePoems.htm.

Rosenberg, J. (n.d.). Columbine massacre. Downloaded 26 November 2012, http://history1900s.about.com/od/famouscrimesscandals/a/columbine.htm.

Roussouw, M. (2010, 6 March). Right royal protocols for Zuma's stay. *Mail and Guardian.*

Said, E. (1978). *Orientalism. Western Conceptions of the Orient.* London: Penguin.

Sapa, A.P. (2010, 25 June). They can't ban my mind, says cartoonist. *Star.*

Saunders, C. (2010, 8 March). Zuma may be a polygamist but he does not chop off heads. Letter to the press. *Star.*

Sidley, K. (2010, 14 March). Lighting up with lit. *Sunday Times.*

Spender, S. (1932). My parents kept me from children who were rough. Downloaded 2 November 2012, www.learn.hackney.ac.uk/mod/resource/view.php?id=73368&redirect.

Stepney, R. (1994, 14 to 20 October). Egg and sperm race—who's the runner? *Weekly Mail and Guardian.*

Sting. (2003). *Broken Music: A Memoir.* Cambridge: Cambridge University Press.

Stucki, S. The Music Lesson. In L. Christensen (2000). *Reading, Writing and Rising Up.* Milwaukee: Rethinking Schools.

Taylor, O. (2005) quoted by K. Hamilton, (2005). The dialect dilemma. *Black Issues in Higher Education*, 21 April, 34–36.

Topo, G. (2009). Ten years later, the real story behind Columbine. Downloaded 26 November 2012, http://usatoday30.usatoday.com/news/nation/2009-04-13-columbine-myths_N.htm.

The DMOVTON. (2010, 4 March). 100% Zulu boy. *City Press.*

Thompson, J. B. (1990). *Ideology and Modern Culture.* Oxford: Basil Blackwell.

Vargas, J. A. (2010, 25 June). *Time*, 20–21.

Wainainina, B. (1992). How to write about Africa. *Granta* 92. Kenya. Downloaded 2 November 2012, www.granta.com/Archive/92/How-to-Write-about-Africa/Page.

Zapiro. (2010, 5 March). What we have built so quickly is a testament to our real commitment. *Mail and Guardian.*